Sigmund

Freud

Key figures in Counselling and Psychotherapy
Series editor: Windy Dryden

The books in this series provide concise introductions to the life, work and influence of leading innovators whose theoretical and practical contributions have shaped the development of contemporary counselling and psychotherapy. The series includes the following titles:

Sigmund

Freud

Second Edition

Michael Jacobs

SAGE Publications
London • Thousand Oaks • New Delhi

First edition published 1992. Reprinted 1993, 1995, 1997, 1998, 2000,
2002 This edition published 2003

SAGE Publications Ltd
6 Bonhill Street
London EC2A 4PU

SAGE Publications Inc
2455 Teller Road
Thousand Oaks, California 91320

SAGE Publications India Pvt Ltd
B-42, Panchsheel Enclave
Post Box 4109
New Delhi 110 017

British Library Cataloguing in Publication data

A catalogue record for this book is available
from the British Library

ISBN 0 7619 4109 6
ISBN 0 7619 4110 X (pbk)

Library of Congress Control Number: 2002110085

Typeset by C&M Digitals (P) Ltd, Chennai, India
Printed in Great Britain by TJ International Ltd, Padstow, Cornwall

Contents

Preface to the Second Edition

I am keen, as the reader will soon detect, that Freud should occupy the central place in this book, and that, as far as possible, his own writing should provide the material upon which his arguments stand or fall. Like many a reader who has opened one of Freud's books, I have found myself fascinated by his ideas, by the range of his thinking and by the liveliness of his style. Knowing that students to whom I have introduced Freud's own books have similarly been excited and often captivated by him, I have no wish to delay the reader from the main body of my text.

It is important to draw attention to three conventions, which I have found necessary to adopt, arising from the vast literary output by Freud and about Freud. I have drawn upon so many of his papers and books that it has proved impossible to reference in any way other than the Standard Edition's classification of dates of Freud's publications. Even though I do not cite every work, any suffix system of my own would only have made for confusion. The suffix letters added to the dates of publication therefore refer to the bibliography in his Collected Works. As I was rewriting this edition the publication of the new translations of Freud's major works in Penguin Classics gave me the opportunity to refer to the volumes already in print, as well as drawing attention in the Appendix to other volumes still to appear. Those that I have been able to obtain have been used for quotations in preference to the Standard Edition, much of which has been published in the Penguin Freud Library. It will be clear which version I have used from the references in full that follow the Appendix. Another major publishing event since the publication of the first edition of this book has been the production of the Standard Edition in paperback (Virago, 2001). This has made much more accessible for the first time in paperback Freud's papers on technique, which had not been selected for the Penguin Freud Library. They also appeared in the new Penguin Classics translations, in time for me to include those translations in my text. The full details in the References again make the relevant source clear, particularly where page numbers are significant.

I have had to make two further decisions about spelling. I have chosen to standardize the spelling of 'psychoanalysis' and its derivatives, even if in some of the titles and texts cited the original author or editor preferred 'psycho-analysis'. I have done this on the grounds that it is the more common of the two forms, and is used throughout the Penguin Freud Library and Penguin Classics (although not in the Standard Edition).

It has been more difficult to know what to do about the alternative spellings of 'phantasy' and 'fantasy'. There is a British psychoanalytic convention that has used 'phantasy', although more modern books prefer 'fantasy'. The difference may be important: 'phantasy' was originally used to distinguish internalized (private) imaginative constructions and ideas, wishes or fears; 'fantasy' was used of 'externalized' (public) inventions such as fairy stories, science fiction and so on. For example, Freud's death instinct might be called a 'fantasy', an invention (of sorts), whereas his belief in the constant resistance to his ideas might be called a 'phantasy'. I have decided in this edition against adopting the convention, and have used 'fantasy' except in quotations, where I have preserved the form used in the original.

I am grateful to the editor of this series, Windy Dryden, for initially providing me with the opportunity to take Freud as a subject, and the consequent necessity of some disciplined reading – it is all too easy with such a figure as Freud to describe him, his theory or his practice from a less informed position, and from what others have written about him. To discover, as I have often done, that Freud had not *quite* put things the way I imagined he had, has been always refreshing, and at times it has been a revelation. I have tried to be careful to understand Freud before trying to pass on any of his ideas to the reader.

Since the first edition I have retired from the University of Leicester, and am fortunate to share both my leisure in Dorset and my reduced programme of work with my wife, Moira Walker, whose healthy criticism of Freud's more doubtful ideas, and openness to my explanations of what Freud might have meant enlivened the writing of the first edition. The first edition was especially for her, and my first grandchild, Laura. This second edition is likewise for Moira, with thanks for her continued love and support; but Joshua will, I am sure, as my second grandchild, want to be mentioned alongside his sister!

Michael Jacobs
Swanage, August 2002

Acknowledgement

Lines from 'In Memory of Sigmund Freud' are from *Collected Poems* by W.H. Auden, edited by Edward Mendelson (London: Faber and Faber Ltd, 1976). Reprinted with permission of Faber and Faber Ltd (London), Random House Inc (New York) and Curtis Brown Ltd (New York).

1

The Life of Sigmund Freud

For every day they die
among us, those who were doing us some good,
who knew it was never enough but
hoped to improve a little by living.

W.H. Auden: 'In Memory of Sigmund Freud'

An Independent Existence?

'Get it out, produce it, make something of it – *outside you*, that is;
give it an existence independently of you.' Such was Freud's
advice to Joan Riviere, one of his English translators, and at one
time his analysand (Riviere, 1958: 146). He was referring to a
psychoanalytic explanation which she had shared with him. In
saying this, Riviere felt that he was referring to his own approach
to thinking, to put it on paper or, again in his words, to 'get it out
of your system'.

Freud certainly got much out of his system, in more senses than
one, since it can fairly be claimed, by supporter or critic alike, that
much of what he 'discovered' came from his attempts to understand himself. But both the volume of what he got out, as well as
the very nature of that enterprise of which he hinted to Riviere,
leads the present author to wish it was as straightforward as that
to write about a man whose ideas are so bound up with his own
and with our own existence. To give Freud an independent existence in the mind of the reader is certainly my aim; but the task
presents a number of dilemmas which cast necessary doubts upon
the independence of the enterprise.

That there should be complexities in studying the life and work
of Freud is appropriate for an understanding of a man who, in his
own words, desired 'to understand some of the mysteries of this
world' (Freud, 1927a/2002: 165). Some of these complications are
not peculiar to Freud, and indeed face the student of any major
contributor to scientific or artistic culture. The volume of material by

Freud and on Freud is sufficient to make the task of independent assessment impossible but for the single-minded academic. The British Standard Edition contains twenty-three volumes of Freud's Collected Works plus an index and bibliography, and there are a further five volumes of his short papers. The correspondence between Freud and Fliess, between Freud and Jung, and between Freud and many others fills a further number of books (for example, McGuire, 1974; Masson, 1985; Freud, E., 1961). There are comprehensive and ever more fully resourced biographies, perhaps the best of which is by Peter Gay, most of which run to hundreds of pages (Jones, 1964; Roazen, 1979; Clark, 1980; Gay, 1989). Books written by both followers and critics of psychoanalysis and Freud run into thousands. Even the average university library, where academic psychology is more likely to be critical of Freud than concerned with studying him at any depth, displays more yards of Freudian spine than that generated by the work of any other psychologist. Since this literature – what one might almost call this literary phenomenon – continues to grow year by year, it is no wonder that the potential student of Freud, looking for a pathway through the intellectual industry spawned by this man and his thought, opts for any slim volume that seeks to summarize the central points; and so is encouraged the production of yet more books on Freud.

This volume cannot stand independently of that vast corpus of knowledge and hypothesis. One of my aims is to introduce the reader to literature which could take as much of one's time to absorb as one may wish, including Freud's collected work in the Standard Edition. But even if acquaintance with Freud will be for most readers relatively small, some knowledge of him is essential for any student of the human mind. It is impossible for counsellors or therapists particularly to ignore the influence of this vast amount of material, often understood only in popular form, upon those who come as clients. A historian does not have to be a Catholic, Protestant or even a Christian to study sixteenth-century Europe, but he or she would be a poor scholar without knowledge of reformation and counter-reformation theology, so important was its influence on the culture of that era. Similarly, therapists do not have to be Freudians to practise therapy; but they will be poorly informed if they remain unaware of the impact of Freudian thinking, right or wrong, for good or ill, on twentieth-century Western culture, and therefore upon their clients as well. Indeed, one of the difficulties we now experience, especially when we find apparent confirmation of Freud's ideas in what clients say, is that we can never be sure whether what we observe is genuinely the same as that which Freud also identified, or whether people have been so influenced by his writing (even through the popular press) that they have unconsciously come to express themselves using his concepts. Momigliano (1987) recounts how 'there was [in Vienna] in 1925 not a single high-society or intellectual salon where people were not asking each other about their Oedipus complexes or interpreting each other's slips or parapraxes'. Such informal self- or mutual analysis is no less prevalent in even wider circles today.

I believe that, despite their inevitable shortcomings, Freud's observations, his theories and his guidelines for practice can still make a significant contribution to current counselling and therapy. This is obvious to any psychodynamic therapist, but I have suffi- cient confidence in Freud to think that some of his ideas can also enlighten other schools of therapy, most of which have in large part developed out of, or in differing degrees in reaction to, Freudian theory and practice. I trust I introduce enough of Freud's own writing, albeit selectively, to take the reader behind my own understanding of him, so that I can cut a swathe through the millions of words written for or against Freud, in order to try and reach the man himself. It is this aspect of Freud, the thinker who strove to get his ideas out of himself and to give them independent existence, which is probably the most important aspect of him, as much today as when he wrote. It is that quest for understanding – even though his understanding has in some respects since been shown to be time-bound – which still appeals to many therapists and clients, who likewise may puzzle about what makes them the persons they are. It is that aspect of puzzling over mysteries that remains his lasting legacy in the field of therapy. Others have contributed significantly to the development of therapeutic rela- tionships and to a variety of alternative techniques, but few have persistently asked questions about the nature and origins of persons. Counselling and therapy are often so concerned with the immediacy of the here-and-now, and with cure and relief, that deeper implications for understanding persons often receive little attention. Although Freud developed a series of techniques which have proved generally valuable in the conduct of therapy, he him- self came to feel that the importance of psychoanalysis was much more in its attempts to discover the working of the human mind and of the world than in its effectiveness as a means of therapy (Freud, 1924f: 181; 1940a: 416).

We know that Freud began on the path to this large canvas by puzzling long over the smaller and more personal one of his own thoughts, dreams, fantasies and life history. It was 'hard work, at once exhilarating and frustrating' (Gay, 1989: 98). Through all that he wrote – even if at first much of it seems to be couched in quasi-scientific terms – there is something of his own life to be read. There remain, of course, many mysteries about some of Freud's more private inner experiences. As Barron et al. (1991: 143) suggest, 'Freud's passionate attempts to uncover secrets ran like a leitmotiv throughout his life' and as such are linked to his character, which 'reveals paradoxical attitudes: openness towards sharing information of a personal nature in order to advance psychoanalysis yet pronounced secretiveness about his private life, in particular his personal history and his marital life'. But as Freud writes we catch glimpses both of him, and at times what it might have been like to be with him in his consulting room. Certainly there is nowhere else quite like his essays and lectures for finding such a fresh, witty, clear and persuasive picture of his thinking and his style.

It is partly because Freud tried in his many papers and books to give his ideas an 'independent existence' that his writing to some extent hides the inner Freud from us. His wish to be remembered more for his ideas than for himself has led to obvious difficulties for his biographers, since he was eager to destroy some of the private documents which might otherwise have added to the biographer's resources. In 1885, for example, 'I have destroyed all my notes of the last fourteen years, as well as letters, scientific extracts and manuscripts of my works' (Gay, 1989: xiii). This exercise was repeated several times in his life. Some of his correspondence and many other papers must have been lost. Furthermore, some of his private letters and papers were embargoed at the request of their donors, although by 1992 over 80 per cent of the Freud Archives had been derestricted, and made available to scholars at the Freud Museum, London, or the Library of Congress, Washington (Blum, 1992).

Freud may appear to offer assistance to those who would understand him as a person in his short work *An Autobiographical Study* (1925d), but its title is something of a misnomer. It is more (in his own words, in which the reader will note his use of the third person) 'an account of his personal share in the development of psychoanalysis' (1925d: 186). There are some dates, some places, and there are names of those who influenced his intellectual development. But personal material, such as the influence of his upbringing and his family relationships, is kept to a minimum. Riviere refers to Freud as a man of 'dignity and reserve', although not retiring or withdrawn. There was a modesty about him that one might expect of one living in an age which had tried to keep under wraps much that he later uncovered through his meticulous work with his patients. Although he at times appeared to refer to such great leaders as Napoleon or Moses as if in some way he wished to identify with them, Riviere comments that 'he did not appear especially interested in impressing himself on people or seeking to convince others of his views'. Nevertheless she adds that he 'developed this special capacity for presenting his conclusions as if he were bent on enabling the reader to take them in' (1958: 145–6). Her feeling is that he did this by creating a body of knowledge outside himself, independent of himself, but (we may add) sometimes at the expense of our knowing him better.

Yet there is another side to this apparent modesty and reluctance to reveal himself. In the autobiographical study Freud rejects any claim the public may have 'to learn any more of my personal affairs – of my struggles, my disappointments and my successes' (1925d: 258). In the next sentence he points out that he has 'in any case been more open and frank in some of my writings … than people usually are who describe their lives for their contemporaries or for posterity. I have had small thanks for it, and from my experience I cannot recommend anyone to follow my example.' He was referring here especially to *The Interpretation of Dreams* (1900a) and to *The Psychopathology of Everyday Life* (1901b/2002), where many of the examples he gives are drawn from his own dreams, from his own past and his own daily experiences. It is easy to forget the many years which Freud spent in self-analysis: it was from himself that he drew the material with which he created his first interpretations of human experience, although his stress on the value of the analyst, as a second person interpreting resistance in the patient inevitably leads us to question the degree of objectivity that can be achieved in and through self-analysis. Not surprisingly, biographers also draw upon those same dreams and memories in their own attempts to analyse Freud. Thus there have been different attempts by writers (particularly those who are also analysts) to reinterpret Freud's famous dream of 'Irma's injection', to understand for example the significance and nature of Freud's relationship with his close correspondent and friend in the 1890s, Wilhelm Fliess. Or the biographer who turns Freud's own methods upon Freud can inevitably find examples of Freud's own slips of the pen, such as the letter to Jung where Freud turns a lower case 'i' into a capital 'I' (in German). Gay suggests that this turns Freud's wish to 'thrash them [opponents]' into a 'thrash you', showing his 'suppressed uneasiness' to his younger associate (1989: 213).

The discriminating reader is therefore presented with frequent opportunities of insight into the apparently self-contained Freud, even though the references are abbreviated and at times self-censored versions of the more rigorous analysis that Freud brought to his past memories and present experiences. What makes the study of Freud peculiar is the way we use his own ideas and theories to study him, as if we had totally absorbed his method, whatever our reservations about the lengths to which he appears to take some interpretations. Just as his studies of great figures such as Leonardo da Vinci and Michelangelo demonstrate the impossibility for him of separating art from the artist, so we cannot, even if Freud desired it otherwise, give his ideas independent existence; nor can this chapter on his life be seen as straightforward factual biography. He has taught us a particular type of enquiry: who or what made him the man he was, producing the ideas which he did?

In asking such questions (as most biographers now do, whoever their subject) we may therefore appear to play straight into Freud's hands: we immediately seem to affirm the correctness of his ideas by using them to gain deeper understanding of his life and of his theories. Such circularity of thinking is displeasing to the philosopher, the logician and the scientist, even if it makes some sense to the artist. It is a form of narcissism, holding a mirror to Freud in which he reflects himself. There is even a kind of incestuousness inherent in the exercise – although by using such terms as 'narcissism' and 'incestuous' I here again betray the way Freud's thinking, whether it is right or wrong, has got under our collective skin, and emerges in much of our critical language. Although we have to make a conscious effort to avoid uncritical dependence upon Freudian terms, it is impossible to escape the particular insight he has stressed, that there is a dynamic between a person's life and a person's attitudes, and between their work and their inner needs. Another dynamic is the way in which past experience, and the interpretation we put upon such experience, influences our current interpretation of present experience.

It is not my brief or my intention to convince the reader of the correctness of any or all of Freud's theories. There is no reason to assume that particular interpretations which Freud put upon his own and others' experiences are accurate. But I am aware that it is impossible for me even to embark upon a summary of his life and work without looking for explanations of the kind which Freud's influence has taught our present culture to seek.

Biographies of Freud often interweave details of his theory and practice as they developed chronologically, together with accounts of the other major figures around him. His developing theory I reserve for the second chapter, and his technique for the third. I intend to say little about other major figures, although some of them merit their own volumes in this series (Segal, 1992; Jacobs, 1995;

Casement, 2001). In this chapter, bearing in mind the reservations already expressed, I describe Freud's childhood and his professional life, asking how those early years might have influenced his later thinking. It is important to remember that the cultural background also plays a major part: there is the question of Freud's Jewishness as well as the anti-Semitic climate in Vienna; but again I reserve these and many of the major intellectual influences on Freud for the next chapter.

His Early Life

Freud describes his origins thus: 'I was born on 6 May 1856, at Freiberg in Moravia, a small town in what is now Czechoslovakia. My parents were Jews, and I have remained a Jew myself' (1925d: 190). His family moved to Vienna when he was four years old, and he remained there until 1938, when he and his psychoanalyst daughter Anna were given permission to leave the Nazi-occupied city. He died in Hampstead, London, on 23 September 1939.

The early reference to his Jewish parentage, as well as another soon afterwards referring to his experience at University of being 'expected to feel myself inferior and an alien because I was a Jew' (1925d: 191), illustrate the importance Freud attached to this aspect of his background, and indicate one of the reasons for his readiness to see rejection of his ideas when the reaction was not in fact always as strong as he made out. He writes of himself: 'The question may be raised whether the personality of the present writer as a Jew who never sought to disguise the fact that he is a Jew may not have had a share in provoking the antipathy of his environment of psychoanalysis' (1925e: 273). Being Jewish featured equally strongly in a recollection of his father telling him, when Freud was about eleven years old, of walking in Galicia when a Christian knocked Freud's father's cap into the mud and shouted 'Jew, get off the pavement.' When Freud asked his father what had happened, his father said that he had gone into the road and picked up his cap. Freud's shame at his father's reaction he later contrasted with his own wish to take vengeance. This memory provides rich material for all kinds of interpretations, one of which is Freud's wish to create a system acceptable to the gentile world. 'From his childhood days on, an assertive display of intellectual independence, controlled rage, physical bravery and self-respect as a Jew coalesced into a highly personal, indestructible amalgam in Freud's character' (Gay, 1989: 12). Some even suggest that 'the incident with its emotional swing against the father may well help to explain the genesis of the Oedipus complex' (Clark, 1980: 13).

Other snapshots of Freud's childhood similarly give rise to speculation about the influence of various incidents upon his later theories, although some of his memories have since been shown to be inaccurate, and based largely upon his dreams in later life. Among the memories are feelings of real infantile jealousy upon the birth of his baby brother, born just over a year after Freud yet dying within a few months, leaving Freud feeling the seeds of guilt; a recollection of himself aged about two years old with a boy cousin stealing a bunch of flowers from a little girl; and an oblique hint that it was a nursemaid who initiated Freud in sexual matters when he was about two and a half, 'the primary originator' of his neurosis (Bonaparte et al., 1954: 219). Freud lost the love of this nursemaid when she was arrested for theft and sent to prison, at about the same time that Freud's mother was confined in pregnancy with his sister; and in 'losing' two mother figures at the same time he was confused about what might have happened to them.

At around the same time as Freud remembered it (although we know that it must have been later, when he was about four), Freud remembered his sexual wishes being aroused towards his mother, when he saw her naked in their sleeping compartment during an overnight railway journey. If that seems to our own enlightened age scarcely a startling experience, a measure of just how forbidden such a sight was is conveyed by Freud's use of Latin terms instead of German – Freud writes the words 'matrem' and 'nudam'. Bearing in mind that this incident was recorded in a private letter to his friend Fliess, 'it is no less telling that even at forty-one, already the most unconventional of explorers in the forbidden realms of sexuality, Freud could not bring himself to describe this exciting incident without lapsing into safe distancing Latin' (Gay, 1989: 11). One final example: when Freud was about seven or eight he urinated in his parents' bedroom, in their presence, and was severely reprimanded by his father, who told him that he would never amount to anything. But this blow to his ambition, or perhaps spur to ambition, was untypical. Freud was a favourite son who could do little wrong.

There are other facets to his family of origin which may be relevant to understanding his later ideas. His father, for example, was old enough to be his grandfather, and Freud was the first son of his father's third wife. This young woman – 'young and beautiful' as Freud writes – was about the same age as Freud's half-brother Philip, and Freud's 'nephew' was one year older than Freud. In age at least Philip seemed a more suitable partner for his mother than Freud's elderly father.

What is particularly interesting is that Freud in his self-analysis concentrated less upon his mother, and principally upon his father. Part of the reason for this may have been the impact upon him of his father's death; but the lack of attention paid to the influence upon him of his mother must be attributable (at least in Freudian terms) to some resistance on Freud's part. There is only scanty material available on Amalie Freud, but Carvalho suggests that a gentle, rather ineffective father may have exposed Freud to an 'all-too-present mother' (1982: 343). In a study of the influence of his mother upon Freud's thought, Estelle Roith says that Amalie was difficult to live with, 'complaining', a 'tyrant', a 'disciplinarian', and 'authoritarian' (Roith, 1987: 110–11). She observes that Freud's essays on femininity were only written after his mother's death. Orgel (1996: 47) also suggests that 'the death of his mother seemed to ease his dread of identifying with her, to free him to acknowledge heretofore neglected aspects of the little boys' early relationships to their mothers and women; he could begin to consider in new ways how the subjective experience of girls and women overlapped those of boys and men'. Gay too comments that Freud 'never fully worked through the meaning of his passionate unconscious ties to that commanding figure' (1989: 11), and suggests this as one of the reasons why women remained such a dark and obscure subject for him. Barron et al. (1991: 151) summarize their description of Freud and his mother in similar vein:

> Freud's temperamental, wilful, demanding mother selected him as her golden child. Her commitment to him was restricted by her continuous childbearing, and her surrendering of his care to a surrogate mother, his nurse. He was jealous of his first sibling and fearful, because, taken by death, Julius had vanished. To that frightful tragedy was added the sudden disappearance of his nurse just at the time of his mother's confinement and delivery of her next child, Anna. He was now deeply bereft and greatly confused about who was father of whom. His oedipal development confronted him with more riddles than Oedipus himself faced.

Freud's education was at the Viennese equivalent of a British grammar school, where 'I was at the top of my class for seven years' (1925d: 190). His schooling, typical of that time, gave him a classical education and included Greek mythology, philosophy and literature. Freud was always very well read and immersed in the arts as much as the sciences. His father insisted that Freud should follow his own inclinations in respect of choice of profession although Freud writes: 'neither at that time, nor indeed in my later life, did I feel any particular predilection for the career of a doctor' (1925d: 190). Indeed, his first ambition was to study law although the attraction of Darwin's theories, then of topical interest, and an essay on Nature, which Freud heard read in public shortly after his seventeenth birthday, 'decided me to become a medical student' (1925d: 191). Such at least are the two reasons Freud gives, although the motives for his choice are rather harder to unravel. Two of the impulses that cannot be excluded, suggests Gay, were 'the need for revenge and self-vindication', while he quotes Freud as saying that he was also moved by 'a greed for knowledge' (1989: 23). Barron et al. (1991: 144) interpret how, in the essay Freud heard, 'nature is portrayed here as a seductress – fickle, mysterious, unyielding, powerful, capable of great love for "her favourites".'

Freud's university career led him through philosophy and zoology, but with medicine winning out in the end. Yet he was never happy with 'the various branches of medicine proper, apart from psychiatry' (1925d: 192). For over six years he therefore worked in research laboratories, taking his Doctor of Medicine in 1881. During the time spent on research Freud studied the central nervous system in fish as well as the sexual organs of the common eel. He was able to work with and learn from some of the greatest authorities in Vienna. This was also the point at which he met his first collaborator, Josef Breuer. Freud's earliest published papers date from this time, and 'detail findings that are far from trivial' (Gay, 1989: 36), although several times he failed to see some of his research through far enough to earn the honour of major achievement. His biographer Ernest Jones comments 'that Freud narrowly missed world fame in early life through not daring to pursue his thoughts to their logical – and not far-off – conclusion' (Gay, 1989: 36).

It was from 1882 onwards that Freud took the step that was in the end to bring him such fame. In that year he moved from the shelter of the laboratory to the living and complex world of the general hospital. He met his future wife, Martha Bernays, and was engaged to her within two months, so that earning a better living now became a high priority. But first he set off on an intellectual and geographical tour that was to provide him with the new directions that were needed for the development of psychoanalysis.

Studying in Paris

For three years Freud moved round different departments in the General Hospital in Vienna. He became interested in the properties of cocaine, and began taking the drug both as a stimulant when depressed and to help him to relax in social settings. The cocaine episode is one example of his failure to pursue his ideas: good humouredly Freud would cite his negligence in not publishing his discovery of the anaesthetic properties of cocaine. An associate, to whom he introduced this idea, instead became known as the discoverer of the local anaesthetic. There is no evidence that he became addicted to it, although his lifelong passion for cigars, which must have contributed to his cancer, has all the marks of dependency upon tobacco. He himself thought that smoking was a substitute for masturbation, although the anecdote about Freud alighting from a train smoking a cigar and responding to the onlookers' smiles by saying 'A cigar is *also* a cigar', shows he recognized the place of the concrete alongside the symbolic. (Yet, as Josephs observes, 'once having entered the Freudian universe, it becomes extremely difficult to take things at face value once again: a cigar can never be just a cigar' (1989: 498).

In 1885 Freud was appointed Lecturer in Neuropathology at the University in Vienna on the strength of his clinical publications; and, with the assistance of a bursary, travelled to Paris to study under Charcot, Professor of Neuropathology. The importance of Charcot's work to Freud lay in a number of directions. Charcot was using hypnosis seriously – often thought of as merely a theatrical entertainment – to induce and cure symptoms such as paralysis of limbs and senses. By doing so, Charcot was able to show that these so-called 'hysterical phenomena' (or conversion hysteria) were genuine complaints of a psychological origin, and were neither signs of malingering nor of organic dysfunctioning: hysteria had been thought to be connected with the womb, and despite the evidence for it, the possibility of hysteria in men was dismissed because men had no womb. 'What mattered most to Freud was that [Charcot] was obviously prepared to take his patients' outlandish behaviour seriously, and no less prepared to entertain strange hypotheses' (Gay, 1989: 51). It was also important for Freud that Charcot supported practice in preference to theory and observed that 'theory is all very well, but that does not prevent facts from existing' (Gay, 1989: 51). Freud never forgot this.

There are three other ways in which Charcot influenced the development of Freud's thinking. The first is the obvious significance that the effects of hypnotic suggestion have for the power of the unconscious. The second was a possible 'side-effect' from the use of hypnosis, the attachment of the patient to the doctor, a 'magnetic passion' sometimes filial, sometimes maternal or sometimes erotic love. This phenomenon was to have great bearing on Freud's development of the concept of transference. Thirdly, Charcot suggested in Freud's mind some sort of link between sexuality and neurosis. At a reception at Charcot's house Freud had overheard his host excitedly arguing about a case: '*dans des ças pareils c'est toujours la chose génitale, toujours – toujours – toujours'* ('in such cases it is always a question of the genitals – always – always – always'). Freud wondered why Charcot never said this publicly (1914d: 71).

First Steps towards Psychoanalysis

Freud returned to Vienna to put his rudimentary learning into practice, using hypnosis to relieve the symptoms of the patients who were referred to him. He married in 1886, and set up in private practice in order to support himself and his wife. They were to have six children over the next nine years, the last being Anna, who later became Freud's principal interpreter, as well as a pioneer of child therapy in her own right. Freud's wife Martha was more a *hausfrau* than an intellectual companion, the latter role being taken by her sister Minna, who was Freud's second close confidante (the first being the German doctor Fliess) during the lonely years of the 1890s. Minna lived with the Freuds continuously from the mid-1890s. Rumours of an affair between Freud and Minna (started by Jung, some suggest as a projection of his own affair with Sabina Spielrein) are examined at length in Gay's biography (1989: 752–3) and for the time being dismissed by him. Gay hints at the frustration of having to wait for the release of Freud's correspondence for further evidence on this and other of Freud's relationships; as indeed another biographer, Clark, does with reference to Freud's relationship with Fliess. The release of the Freud–Minna Bernays correspondence in the 1990s appears not to have substantiated any case for impropriety.

Freud's private work brought him opportunities to develop his practice as well as his theory. During this time of experiment, his relationship with the older man, Josef Breuer, and the lesser man (intellectually) Wilhelm Fliess, were crucial for his thinking about psychoanalysis (a term he first used in 1896). With the former he discussed his work with patients, with the latter he embarked upon a correspondence which ran into many hundreds of letters, and which provided Freud with a sounding-board for his self-analysis (Masson, 1985). Fliess' preoccupation with numerology and other bizarre theories of periodicity may not have made him an obvious choice as an intellectual companion, but he provided 'understanding, stimulation and support' during the years when Freud was using methods and developing ideas that 'at best were controversial and at worst were anathema to the medical establishment' (Clark, 1980: 97). Fliess speculated about infantile sexuality and the idea of bisexuality before Freud, although it was Freud who first proposed the sexual origins of neuroses.

Many writers have commented on the intense transference relationship that Freud appears to have made with Fliess. Freud's famous dream of Irma's injection, which he interpreted as a wish to protect himself against the charge of supposed professional negligence, is understood by many later interpreters as a wish to protect Fliess from accusations of professional irresponsibility. In reality Fliess had been called in by Freud to operate upon a young woman suffering from nosebleeds. It was later discovered, when the patient nearly died from further bleeding, that Fliess had left half a metre of gauze in the wound. Freud tried to exonerate Fliess from blame in subsequent correspondence, and in the dream every doctor involved *except* Fliess is blamed. The explanation given by Freud in *The Interpretation of Dreams* (1900a: 180–99), as well as some of his explanations of the young woman's continued suffering as hysterical and attention-seeking, demonstrate that Freud is not immune from self-deception, and that in protecting Fliess he misinterpreted both himself and his patient. Two of his biographers, however, draw attention to a sentence in *The Interpretation of Dreams* which suggests that Freud may have begun to see some of these other implications in the dream, but was not prepared to put them in print (Clark, 1980: 146–52; Gay, 1989: 80–7).

The break from Fliess (one of many that were to follow in the years ahead from close companions) took place much later. But the first break was from Breuer. Freud and Breuer co-authored *Studies on Hysteria* (1895d), a reflection of their co-operative work on cases during the 1880s and early 1890s. Four of Freud's cases follow a single example of Breuer's, although Freud alludes to many other cases in passing. It is in fact Breuer's case dating back to the early 1880s, that of a young woman introduced to the reader as 'Anna O', which must count as the first case in the history of psychoanalysis. Breuer learned much from it, which he shared with Freud. But he also failed in some respects, and left sufficient loose ends to enable Freud to weave together what he had learned from Charcot and from his own self-analysis into a new theory of the origin of hysteria, and a new formulation of handling the therapeutic relationship. 'In confiding to his young friend Freud the fascinating story of Anna O., [Breuer] generated more unsettling ideas in Freud than he himself was willing to entertain' (Gay, 1989: 63).

Anna O. (Freud and Breuer, 1895d: 73–102) presented a variety of symptoms: partial paralysis, disturbances of vision, hallucinations, speech difficulties, even a hint of multiple personality. The symptoms appeared to have been precipitated by the fatal illness of her father, whom Anna O. had nursed for all but the last two months of his life. This attachment of young Viennese women to their fathers, including their nursing of them, appears in other cases as well, and demonstrates the significance Freud was to give to the intimate feelings between parent and child. Anna O. was seen daily by Breuer, often when she was in a state of self-hypnosis. She herself described these times, when she spoke and Breuer listened, as her 'talking cure' or as 'chimney sweeping'. She referred especially here to the cathartic effect of being able to recall memories and to discharge emotions that she was unable to get in touch with in her normal waking self. This discharge of memories and the intense feeling attached to them were called respectively 'abreaction' and 'catharsis' (1895d: 59).

Breuer recognized that under hypnosis Anna could be helped to trace the origins of each of her symptoms. He reported towards the end of the case that 'she regained her mental balance entirely' (1895d: 95). We know now, however, that Breuer brushed over the fact that her cure was not complete, as well as glossing over his difficulties in acknowledging that some of the more florid symptoms in the case were sexual in origin. A further missing element was supplied by Freud many years later. In a letter written in 1932 Freud reported that Breuer had told him that on the evening that all of Anna's symptoms had apparently been brought under control, she experienced hysterical abdominal cramps and had talked of expecting Breuer's child. Anna's fantasy was too much for Breuer, who seems to have sewn up the case there and then, referring her elsewhere. Freud commented that Breuer held 'the key in his hand' but was unable to use it (Gay, 1989: 67). That key was the phenomenon of 'transference'. The Anna O. case is, as Clark writes, 'a dubious record' but that 'does not affect its significance in the history of psychoanalysis' (1980: 105). Breuer's reaction to his patient opened a door for Freud into a potentially important new method of therapy.

Freud's ability to stay with events such as these, and to try and understand them rather than suppress them, is perhaps the mainstay of his genius. He too listened to his patients, and gradually dropped the use of hypnosis in favour of the 'pressure' technique – laying his hands on the patient's forehead and commanding the answers to various questions about the origins of symptoms. He then learned, again from a patient, that it was better not to ask questions, but simply to listen. Over these early years of experimentation Freud shifted from a medical model of active intervention to a relationship model based on more passive attentiveness to the patient. I suspect that with growing experience and perhaps over-confidence in the correctness of his interpretations Freud sometimes reverted to a more active style, and to the medical model in telling the patient what his or her symptoms or dreams meant. Nevertheless his papers on technique emphasize the key elements that emerged in these early years of experiment: the cardinal rules that the patient should speak freely, without censoring anything (free association), and that the therapist should attend freely in her or his own thoughts. During this early period Freud also recognized that the instruction to 'free associate' could be strongly resisted, and that it was at points of resistance that the most significant memories lay waiting to emerge. The development of Freud's technique, together with his understanding of transference, during these years immediately before and after the publication of *Studies on Hysteria* are examined more fully in Chapter 3.

The Significance of Sexuality

Freud's father died in 1896. This was, according to Gay, 'a profound personal experience from which Freud drew universal implications; it acted like a pebble thrown into a still pond, making successive rings of unsuspected magnitude' (1989: 89). His reflection, through self-analysis, upon his relationship with his father was partially responsible for the emphasis he gave to the Oedipus complex. Gay observes that what matters is not whether Freud had, or imagined that he had, an Oedipus complex, but whether his claim that everyone passes through such a complex can be substantiated. However, Freud 'did not regard his own experiences as automatically valid for all humanity' (Gay, 1989: 90). His work demonstrates an ambivalence in him, with recognition of individuality on the one hand and a tendency towards universalization on the other, the latter perhaps stemming from his wish to establish scientific principles. Freud's case histories read like individual stories, as he himself comments: 'It still strikes me myself as strange that the case histories I write should read like short stories' (Freud and Breuer, 1895d: 231). But he used them to put forward more general hypotheses.

An early illustration of the dangers of universalizing arose from Freud's theory of actual seduction as the cause of hysteria. Speaking to a local group of doctors on the origins of hysteria in 1896 he noted that all eighteen cases that he cited suggested as the cause of their symptoms the sexual abuse of his patients as children. His theory brought scorn upon him, and must have been partly responsible for his revision of the theory of actual seduction as the one explanation of neurosis. But there were other reasons for his change of mind. He was aware, for example, of his own neuroses, and could not accuse his own father of abusing him – although we recall that his nurse may have done so. He therefore repudiated, at first in a letter to Fliess in 1897, and later in print in 1904, the seduction theory as a *general* explanation, replacing it with the explanation that 'these scenes of seduction had never taken place, and that they were only fantasies which my patients had made up or which I myself had perhaps forced on them' (Freud, 1925d: 217).

More recent recognition of the size of the problem of child abuse in turn casts some doubt upon the wisdom of Freud's retraction, and in Chapter 4 I examine the stringent criticism of him for backing down on this point. I also suggest that the criticism is overstated. What he did not retract was the significance of sexuality in the origins of neurosis, examining infantile sexual development in detail in *Three Essays on the Theory of Sexuality* (1905d). Although he was not the first to suggest sexual feelings in childhood, Freud's book – 'as tightly packed as a hand grenade and as explosive' (Gay, 1989: 148) – broke new ground for many of its readers in suggesting the normality of sexual feelings in infancy and childhood. The general opinion of the time (and indeed later) was to put down displays of sexual interest in young children 'as signs of degeneracy or premature depravity or as a curious freak of nature' (Freud, 1925d: 216).

The Growth of Psychoanalysis

The beginning of the next decade and the early years of the twentieth century saw the end of Freud's largely isolated pioneering position, although he looked back on that earlier time as 'like a glorious heroic age' (1914d: 79). Reflecting at another time Freud also saw the publication of *The Interpretation of Dreams* in 1900 as significant: 'psychoanalysis may be said to have been born with the twentieth century' (1925d: 161). Describing that book to Fliess he used the image of the guided tour:

> The whole is laid out like a promenade. At the beginning, the dark forest of authors (who do not see the trees), hopeless, rich in wrong tracks. Then a concealed narrow pass through which I lead the reader – my model dream with its peculiarities, details, indiscretions, bad jokes – and then suddenly the summit and the view and the question, Please, where do you want to go now? (quoted in Gay, 1989: 106)

The Interpretation of Dreams was considered by Freud the most significant of all his works, although it sold very few copies in the years immediately after its publication, and a second edition was not required until 1909. It was reviewed initially in at least eleven journals, although Freud's comment was that it was 'scarcely reviewed' (1925d: 231).

Yet the book attracted attention, as well as followers. The first ten years of the new century saw the slow but gradual development of psychoanalysis as a theory, as a technique and as a movement, from the first meeting of what were to become regular Wednesday night gatherings at Freud's house, where there were five physicians, to the addition of other doctors and a few interested laymen, and then to the formation of the International Congresses in 1908. The same period saw a professorship for Freud, something he had desired for years, and also 'social stature, public resonance, ardent followers, and closet controversies' (Gay, 1989: 136).

It would be tedious to trace here the growing list of followers, some of whom are regarded by psychoanalysts anxious to prove their orthodoxy as a kind of apostolic succession: who analysed whom sometimes assumes unnecessary importance for training analysts. Historians of the psychoanalytic movement have indeed noted the parallels with religion – Freud as the prophetic leader, the arguments over terminology, the orthodox and the heretics, the sectarianism arising from personal and theoretical disagreements (see also Kernberg's criticism of current training for the same reasons, 1996). Bleuler, Jung's senior in Zurich, protested when resigning from the International Psychoanalytic Association: 'This "who is not for us is against us", this "all or nothing" is in my opinion necessary for religious communities and useful for political parties ... but for science I consider it harmful' (Gay, 1989: 215).

Many of those who met with Freud and disputed with each other have their own place in the history of therapy, outside as well as within psychoanalytic circles. Otto Rank, whose work on birth trauma did not win Freud's agreement, was secretary to the Wednesday Society. Alfred Adler was for a while President of the Vienna Psychoanalytic Society, until he and Freud fell out in 1911. Freud described Adler as entirely repudiating the importance of sexuality, tracing back the formation of character and neuroses 'solely to men's desire for power and to their need to compensate for their constitutional inferiorities' (1925d: 236). Such a dismissive description does not do justice to ideas that continued in the development of Adler's Individual Psychology, and re-emerged in the 1930s through the work of neo-Freudians such as Eric Fromm (e.g. 1966) and Karen Horney (Rubins, 1978).

Others played an important part in establishing psychoanalysis in other European cities, as well as making their own contributions to theory and practice: Karl Abraham was a pioneer of psycho-analytic training and practice in Berlin, Sandor Ferenczi in Budapest (Ferenczi and Abraham were in turn Melanie Klein's analysts), Ernest Jones in Canada and later in London. Carl Jung (Casement, 2001) was a similar ambassador in Zurich, although he too was compelled to break away in late 1912.

Jung and Freud first corresponded in 1906. They met in 1907 and soon became friends. Freud liked Jung and envisaged that he would become his successor. Gay comments that Freud 'needed to idealize someone as he had idealized Fliess' (1989: 201). In 1910 Jung was elected president of the International Psychoanalytic Association, although less than three years later had split with Freud completely. The two men had travelled together with other colleagues to the United States in 1909, where Freud was engaged to deliver five public lectures at Clark University, Massachusetts. These lectures, brilliantly delivered and very well received, still express the core elements of psychoanalysis in a clear and attrac-tive form (1910a/2001). It was on the Atlantic voyage that the first seeds of doubt and dissension between him and Jung were sown. Jung had interpreted one of Freud's dreams but needed more details of Freud's private life. Freud objected that he could not be analysed by Jung, because this would put his authority at risk. In Jung's opinion, 'Freud, the self-proclaimed apostle of scientific candor, was placing personal authority above truth' (Gay, 1989: 225). Although Jung seems to have kept up the appearance of still being Freud's loyal 'son' the two disagreed more and more over a variety of matters, principally the ever-divisive issue of sexuality. They differed too over the place of religious ideas and feelings in mental life, Jung believing the spiritual to be an important dimen-sion in mental health. Freud's nineteenth-century positivism had no use for the supernatural and the mystical. Many other factors gradually separated Freud and Jung, as Jung grew more and more bold in his revision of Freudian theory. No doubt other more per-sonal factors also divided them, since they were both powerful men, and creative, independent thinkers. Jung had once written that it was hard to work side by side with the creator. The close-ness between the two, followed by the break that Jung described as a type of liberation, has an Oedipal quality about it, as more than one biographer has noted.

These major disputes wearied Freud. Gay records that Freud confided in Ferenczi concerning the arguments in Vienna that 'it was often more agreeable as long as I was alone' (1989: 221); and the break with Jung wearied him, making him even more pes-simistic and defensive. In such a mood he was prey to Ernest

Jones' plan to form a secret committee, which would rally round Freud against any attempt to break away from the fundamental tenets of psychoanalysis – repression, the unconscious or infantile sexuality. Gay records that Freud liked the idea: 'What took hold of my imagination immediately is your idea of a secret council composed of the best and most trustworthy among our men to take care of the further development of psychoanalysis and defend the cause against personalities and accidents when I am no more' (quoted in Gay, 1989: 230). Freud had started what he called his 'Project', following the publication of *Studies on Hysteria*. With the 'Project' turning gradually into the 'Cause' psychoanalysis became institutionalized, and took a step towards the narrowness of thinking and rigidity of structure that has ultimately weakened it as an organization. Thankfully psychoanalysis was sufficiently influential outside its parent organization for Freud's theory and practice to exercise a positive influence upon the development of psychotherapy and counselling.

The Consequences of War

As serious an issue for Freud, and perhaps more influential in its effect than the infighting within psychoanalysis, was the much greater European conflict now known as the Great War. In the ten years up until 1915 Freud had what Gay calls a 'punishing schedule' of work: his clinical work was arduous – up to eight patients a day for an hour each. He 'published papers on literature, law, religion, education, art, ethics, linguistics, folklore, mythology, archaeology, war, and the psychology of schoolboys' (Gay, 1989: 306). Some of these essays show true brilliance; others verge on the fantastic. He also published further case histories (see the Penguin Freud Library, Volumes 8 and 9 and the Penguin Classics translations) as well as important papers on technique (in Penguin Classics), partly written in an attempt to stem the flood of 'wild analysis'.

Even with such a busy routine, Freud also managed to eat regularly daily with his family, at one o'clock sharp; to play cards; to visit his mother weekly; to walk; to entertain; and occasionally to visit the opera. He accepted invitations to address conferences as well as more popular audiences. He gave public lectures in the University of Vienna, published in an eminently readable text (*Introductory Lectures on Psychoanalysis*) in 1916–17. Every year he ensured proper holidays with his family in the mountains. It is useful to remember that Freud was by now in his late fifties.

The war interrupted all this activity. His three sons were all in action. Psychoanalytic congresses were cancelled, and many of

Freud's followers were called up. He often felt as alone as he had in the first ten years of his psychoanalytic practice. His private practice diminished and his income dropped severely. He passed his sixtieth birthday, nearing, so he thought, the year in which an irrational superstition convinced him he would die. Perhaps the most telling sign of the war's impact on him was his deepening concern for humankind, and a growing pessimism about the ability of human beings to live in civilized society. He published papers on the disillusion of war, and he turned his attention to the subject of death, presaging his formulation of the death drive in the years following the end of the war. He argued that modern man denied the reality of death and had developed ways of softening the impact of the death of others. The Great War had cracked open the veneer of civilization and exposed the degree of aggression buried beneath the surface. It

> stripped us of our later cultural superimpositions, and has let the primeval man within us into the light. ... We recall the old proverb *Si vis pacem, para bellum*. If you want to preserve peace, arm for war. It would be timely to paraphrase it: *Si vis vitam, para mortem*. If you want to endure life, prepare yourself for death. (1915b)

Freud in his late seventies took up this concern for war again in a short correspondence with Einstein (*Why War?*, 1933b).

Nor did things improve following the cessation of hostilities. For more than two years he and his family struggled to survive – food, heating, even paper for writing were scarcely obtainable. Inflation sapped his savings. Freud wrote to his nephew in England complaining about the quality of life. Both he and his wife succumbed for a while in an epidemic of Spanish influenza, which killed thousands in Vienna alone.

Grief, Pain and Death

Freud's salvation came through long hours of work, with numbers of foreign visitors who came for training in psychoanalysis. From 1920 he only took on patients who were in training as analysts, favouring those from abroad because they would be able to take back their understanding of analysis to their home countries, and help spread word of the discipline (Momigliano, 1987: 376). He also needed the stable currencies with which they could afford to pay him, although he, like other analysts in Vienna at the time, also saw two patients per week free (Momigliano, 1987: 382). Work, as Gay observes, was also Freud's way of coping with mourning the death of a large number of people who were close to him, some of course closer than others. There was the suicide of his follower Victor Tausk and the death from cancer of von Freund, a generous supporter of psychoanalytic publications. His daughter Sophie died of influenza, a death that he deeply mourned but never got over. 'It is tempting', writes Gay, 'to read Freud's late psychoanalytic system, with its stress on aggression and death, as a response to his grief of these years' (1989: 394). In *Beyond the Pleasure Principle* (1920g), a difficult text to read, Freud suggested a death drive, analogous to the sexual drive, but in this case representing the return of an organism to its earliest state, that of non-existence. In this book Freud was struggling to come to terms with an explanation for aggression, although he avoided the much more straightforward possibility of an aggressive drive. Of the many analysts influenced by Freud only Melanie Klein really accepted the death instinct in her own attempts to understand hate and aggression (Segal, 1992: 52–3, 97–8).

Perhaps Freud was trying to come to terms with much more. It is tempting to link his wish to work through this idea with thoughts of his own death, although it was not in fact until 1923 that Freud's cancer of the jaw was diagnosed. Even then his wishful thinking made him diagnose his condition himself as being benign; and there was collusion from his closest friends and colleagues, who tried to keep from Freud the seriousness of the cancer. In this at least they did not know him well enough, although they should have surmised the same courage in the face of personal pain that he had shown towards the opposition to his ideas, sometimes within, sometimes outside psychoanalytic circles. Freud was furious when he later heard of their deception.

It was to be a bad year. Freud's young grandson died in June. Freud nearly bled to death after one of his operations. There were two that year, and many others in the years that followed as precancerous growths had to be excised. There were thirty or more minor operations in all, 'to say nothing of the scores of fittings, cleanings, and refittings of Freud's prosthesis ... invasive and irksome procedures', which often hurt him greatly (Gay, 1989: 426–7).

It is against this background of personal pain and discomfort, and other aspects of ageing through his seventies and into his eighties, that the last two decades of Freud's life need to be understood. He had to teach himself to speak again, and the operations also affected his hearing. Yet he continued his practice, and he continued to address a host of issues and ideas, described briefly below. Neither did he give up smoking his favourite cigars, against the advice of his physician Schur, who attended him for the last ten years of his life.

There was another threat to Freud in the rise of Nazi Germany, and in particular in the occupation of Vienna, and the systematic persecution of Jews. High-level diplomatic negotiations took place to get Freud out of Vienna, although it was not easy to persuade the old man to leave the city where he had lived for seventy-eight years. With his daughter Anna he came to London in 1938, living out the last year of his life in Britain, in the home which now houses the Freud Museum. They were months of increasingly torturous pain, although Freud did not lose his sense of humour: when hostilities between Britain and Germany commenced he could still joke with Schur that it would be his last war. It became impossible in the end to relieve his suffering, and even his favourite dog would not come near him. Freud took Schur's hand and reminded him of a contract made ten years previously, that Schur would not let Freud be tormented unnecessarily, and that he was 'not to leave me in the lurch when the time had come'. Schur gave Freud an extra dose of morphine, and repeated this for a further two days. Freud died on 23 September 1939, fulfilling a wish shared nearly forty years before with the Swiss pastor Oskar Pfister: 'no invalidism, no paralysis of one's powers through bodily misery. Let us die in harness' (Gay, 1989: 651).

Anna Freud

During these last twenty years of his life Freud's youngest daughter, Anna, was his closest companion. She had trained as a teacher, but was drawn to her father's profession, becoming one of the early child psychoanalysts. Not only did she become his secretary, and represent him at psychoanalytic congresses when he was unable to attend because of his illness and age; she also assumed his mantle. For many years after his death she was almost literally the living embodiment of Freud, at one and the same time keeping his particular theories centre stage, yet also developing her own thinking and practice, with special attention to the psychology of the ego and to mechanisms of defence; and, more systematically than Freud was able to, tracing certain 'developmental lines' through childhood and adolescence.

It is important to acknowledge Anna Freud in her own right, as a counterbalance to the close (perhaps interdependent rather than dependent) relationship that she had with her father during the last twenty years of Freud's life. In some ways she was in the same position as many of the young women patients in Freud's early analytic practice, because she too nursed her father throughout his operations. She had on occasion to help him fit his prosthesis. She was intimately involved as only mothers and nurses are with all the messiness of the human body. There is no need to ask whether Freud understood the significance of this relationship, since he sometimes spoke of Anna as his Antigone: in classical myth Antigone was the daughter, but also the sister, of Oedipus, who was the companion and guide to her blinded father. Freud seems to have wished that Anna should have separated herself more from him, although he must have known that a conscious intention does not always equal the unconscious wish.

He must assume, of course, some responsibility in hindering Anna from growing up and away from him; he often referred to her as his 'little girl'; and when she wanted to train as an analyst, he not only dissuaded her from studying medicine first, but he also chose to analyse her himself. The analysis began in 1918, and lasted for more than three years; it was taken up again for a year in 1924. This highly controversial procedure was contrary to all the rules of practice that he had laid down, although there was a tendency in Freud not always to observe his own technical guidelines, which will be noticed again in the examination of his technique in Chapter 3. It is at one and the same time a puzzling yet also a redeeming feature in him that someone who at times appears so authoritarian was able to bend his own rules. That does not excuse his decision to analyse his own daughter, although such 'incestuous' therapeutic relationships appear not to have been understood at the time to be potentially damaging. Freud also analysed Ernest Jones' second wife, the two of them corresponding about her health and other matters which would today be felt to be beyond bounds. But then Melanie Klein similarly analysed her own children who were very much younger than Anna, and had little choice in the matter. Freud's biographer Gay also lists Jung (and his wife), Max Graf (and the famous case of his son Little Hans), and Weiss (and his son), as well as Freud's analysis of close friends such as Ferenczi. Freud's verdict on his relationship with Anna was: 'with my own daughter it turned out well' (Gay, 1989: 440). Perhaps her ability to make a name for herself, even while her father was still alive, is confirmatory evidence of this, although the 'entangled relationship', as Gay calls it, clearly also at times caused Freud great distress (1989: 441).

There is a further curious feature in Freud's attitude to women. His difficulty with the psychology of female sexuality and with issues of gender difference is discussed in the next chapter, and some of the criticism of his thinking about women is explored in Chapter 4. In places Freud could write most disparagingly about women; he was not kindly disposed towards the feminist movement, and his picture of women was all too often of 'the sweet competent housewife' (Gay, 1989: 508), and 'the woman who wants to be conquered' (Freud, quoted in Gay, 1989: 508). In common with the male-dominated view of his time Freud could write that 'it seems that women have made few contributions to the discoveries and inventions in the history of civilization' except, he singles out, plaiting and weaving (1933a: 166).

Despite such attitudes, Freud purposefully fostered other women, who wished to train as psychoanalysts, in addition to his daughter Anna. 'Indeed, he undercut his comments on women, which ranged from frank puzzlement to lordly courtesy, by presiding over a profession in which women could rise to the top' (Gay, 1989: 508–9): Anna Freud, Melanie Klein, Lou Andreas-Salome, Helene Deutsch, Joan Riviere, Ruth Mack Brunswick, Marie Bonaparte, Jeanne Lampl-de Groot and Karen Horney are just some of those who made major contributions to psychoanalysis during this last quarter of Freud's life. He did not always agree with the observations that many of these women analysts raised concerning female development, but he gave proper recognition to their questions in his writing, sometimes adding his own doubts (1931b: 389–92). He also accepted that his own experience as an analyst had made it difficult for him to grasp the importance of mothering: his women patients tended to cling to their attachment to father, whereas 'women analysts ... have been able to perceive these facts more easily and clearly because they were helped in dealing with those under their treatment by the transference to a suitable mother-substitute' (1931b: 373). The importance of women 'mothering psychoanalysis' (Sayers, 1991) is a significant feature of this period of Freud's life and of the history of psychoanalysis, which if almost totally missing in the pioneer years nevertheless is obvious following the Great War, in a way that was at the time unique compared to other professions, including medicine.

Later Studies

The psychology of women was just one of many important issues to which Freud's continuously searching mind turned in his old age. Indeed, not only the breadth of his interests but also the publication of so many novel ideas is astonishing for a person of his age and state of health. Where his writing in this period contributes significantly to his theoretical base it is referred to more fully in the next chapter; but the range of subjects to which he turned his mind merits mention: simply putting them together in three paragraphs illustrates the fertility of Freud's thinking.

In the twenty years between the end of the Great War and Freud's death in Hampstead, he examined the relationship between pleasure and reality and postulated the death instinct (1920g). He turned his attention to the phenomenon of the large group in a study of mass psychology (1921c), almost prophetically seeking to understand the same phenomenon that within a few years led to the rise of Hitler, and the loss of individual morality in mass behaviour, not only in mass rallies but in whole nations. He later 'returned to the cultural problems which had fascinated me long before, when I was a youth scarcely old enough for thinking' (1925d: 257): he considered the conflict between the expectations of civilization and the needs and wishes of the individual (1930a/2002). Religious allegiance had formed part of his study of group behaviour. Freud gave further attention to this subject when he examined religion as an illusion (1927c), and again twelve years later becoming more extreme and outspoken in a highly controversial book on the origins of Judaism. Even in the context of much wildly inaccurate speculation, Freud with some justice located the anti-Semitism, which lay behind his motives for the book, in the delusory attitudes in so-called Christian society (1939a).

It must be said that much of what Freud attempted in these studies, some of them only loosely related to his own discipline, remains highly speculative. His knowledge of anthropology, mass psychology and biblical criticism was second-hand, and sometimes revealed his ignorance, risking thereby the complete undermining of his arguments. He at least acknowledged the status of much of this work: in 1935, in a postscript to his autobiography, he wrote that he did not believe that after *The Ego and the Id* (1923b) he made any 'further decisive contributions to psychoanalysis: what I have written on the subject since then has been either unessential or would soon have been supplied by someone else' (1925d: 257). Nevertheless, some of the speculation, even if unproven, remains attractive, and points to the need to go beyond the understanding of individuals to the attempt to investigate behaviour, fantasies and beliefs on a macrocosmic level. Freud thought he perceived that the dynamic conflicts within the individual were reflected in 'the events of human history, the interactions between human nature, cultural development and the precipitates of primeval experiences (the most prominent example of which is religion)' (1925d: 257).

On the level of individual dynamics Freud worked on a major restructuring of his view of the psyche, in which id, ego and superego appeared together for the first time (1923b). He wrote a well argued defence of the training and practice of lay analysts, in which he clearly and confidently explained many of the principles of psychoanalysis to a more popular audience (1926e/2002, 1927a/2002); and he gave further expression to his desire to make psychoanalysis accessible in a second set of public lectures, this time published but not actually delivered (1933a), which brought the former set up to date with reworked versions of many of his current concerns. His autobiography, to which this chapter has often referred, also belongs to this period (1925d), as well as papers on anatomical differences, female sexuality (1931b), the Oedipus complex, resistances to psychoanalysis (1925e/2002), the limitations of psychoanalysis and other aspects of technique. When he died Freud was working on a book in which he was collating *An Outline of Psychoanalysis*, a condensed summary which is more difficult to use than might be apparent from its title (1940a).

Infamy and Fame

That Freud should choose to develop his thinking in these different areas was partly due to the increasing acceptance of his basic tenets and techniques; he was freed of the task of defending psychoanalysis as it increased in popularity. Others could take up its cause, leaving him to consolidate earlier ideas, and to move into new territories of enquiry.

The attention which psychoanalysis, and Freud himself, attracted had its positive and negative sides. In the decade following the Great War, psychoanalysis was hotly debated in fashionable Vienna. It could be described in 1923 as 'not only coloring our literature, but, as a natural result ... creeping into and influencing life in many other directions' (Gay, 1989: 450). Popular judgements and facile opinions took their place alongside more informed criticism, and slanders about Freud as well as misinterpretation abounded. 'The old accusation that Freud was obsessed with sex seemed ineradicable' (Gay, 1989: 451). In America psychoanalytic literature flooded the market: to be in analysis became fashionable. But there was also a great threat to psychoanalysis from quacks, charlatans and money-makers. Another of Freud's biographers, Clark, has described fully (including some amusing as well as serious anecdotes) the impact of Freud's name and ideas on the American press, public, picture houses and psychiatry, as well as the reception of his theories among British intellectuals (1980: 407–22).

Despite his earlier gloomy pessimism about the influence of his ideas Freud had become a household name. Whereas *The Interpretation of Dreams*, published in 1900, had taken years to sell more than a few hundred copies, *Civilization and Its Discontents*, published in 1930, sold out its first edition of 12,000 copies within a year. Within three years, however, Freud's books were being publicly burned in Germany by the Nazis. He commented that in the Middle Ages it would have been he himself who would have been burned; but he cannot have foreseen the irony in that remark, not only in the extermination of so many fellow Jews, but particularly in the deaths of four of his five sisters in various concentration camps.

The popular criticism of psychoanalysis was fuelled by the mavericks, some of whom were enlisted among Freud's supporters. Freud had written against 'wild analysis' in a paper in 1910 (Freud, 1910k/2002), but by the 1920s it was even more prevalent. In America it was possible to be 'psyched' by mail order (Clark, 1980: 408). Alongside unregulated psychoanalysis the official psychoanalytic movement grew, until the Nazi threat decimated it in Germany and Vienna, causing Jewish analysts in particular to emigrate to the United States and Britain. Because the movement itself was gaining strength it sought greater control of standards. There were strong clashes within the International Psychoanalytic Association over the question of whether lay persons could train as analysts. Freud argued strongly in favour of lay analysis, but then he had himself always seen psychoanalysis as a new profession, different from both medicine and the church. He acknowledged quackery, and the concern lest 'lay analysts are responsible for a good deal of mischief and abuse of analysis, and are thereby harming patients as well as the reputatic of analysis' (1927a/2002: 362–3); but he did not feel that strict rules (either from governments or within psychoanalysis itself) were necessary. In the end the differences turned out to be greatest within the international psychoanalytical community. While regulation was perhaps inevitable, training as a psychoanalyst in some countries (such as the United States) was limited to the medical profession. Freud was furious at this, and indeed by this time deeply sceptical of all things American: 'it amounts to a temptation to indulge in repression' (1927a/2002: 363). More generally, the raising of standards also led to increasing narrowness and protectionism, which excluded some of the good as well as the bad.

On a different level, psychoanalysis and its founder Freud began to receive respect, particularly in intellectual circles, both in his own country and internationally. At the opening of the Hebrew University in Jerusalem, Freud's name was listed with Bergson and Einstein as the three men who had most greatly benefited modern thought. In 1930 he was awarded the Goethe Prize for

Literature by the city of Frankfurt: 'This was the climax of my life as a citizen' (1925d: 258). His seventy-fifth birthday saw honours from the Viennese medical establishment, and the unveiling of a plaque at his birthplace. His eightieth birthday saw more tributes, including a congratulatory address signed by many writers and artists; and he had the singular honour of being elected a Corresponding Member of the Royal Society in London. He was delighted to join the ranks of such great scientists as Newton and Darwin, and even more thrilled when, on his arrival in London in 1938, he was personally visited by representatives from the Royal Society, so that he might sign his name in their Charter Book. By contrast Anna Freud notes that Winnicott was the only member of the British Psycho-Analytic Society who called at their home after they had moved to London to ask if they were all right (Rodman, 1987: xix).

Freud's position within European intellectual thought was assured although there is another side to him that should also be recognized. Roazen records that 'his disciples saw Freud as a simple and shy human being who did not intentionally surround himself with the aura of greatness; admiration sometimes embarrassed him, and his lonely simplicity could easily be mistaken for its opposite' (1979: 509). Given the significance which Freud's work has had on relationships, it would be inappropriate to conclude this brief review of Freud's life without at least a glance at the way Freud was perceived by those who knew him.

Freud the Person

As I indicated at the beginning of this chapter, Freud's work suggests a degree of caution is necessary about our ability to be objective, whether about him or any other matter. If perceptions are a combination of what the observer chooses to see as well as what the observed is prepared to reveal, we can expect those who met and worked with Freud to have experienced him in different ways. Thus one patient, known from Freud's case study as the Wolf Man (Freud, 1918b/2002), said in an interview: 'He was a fascinating personality. ... He had very serious eyes that looked down to the very bottom of the soul. ... He had a magnetism or, better an aura that was very pleasant and positive' (Obholzer, 1980: 30). Virginia Woolf (no relation!) commented upon Freud's eyes in a different way (although she met him in the last year of his life), describing him as 'a screwed up shrunk very old man: with a monkey's light eyes'. Yet again, on that same visit Leonard Woolf said of Freud that 'he was extraordinarily courteous in a formal, old fashioned way. ... There was something about him as of a half-extinct volcano, something sombre, suppressed, reserved. He gave me the feeling of great gentleness, but behind the gentleness, great strength' (Gay, 1989: 640). The Woolfs had a fleeting impression. The Wolf Man knew Freud as any long-term patient knows a therapist – very well – but tended to idealize him. Joan Riviere, analysand but also colleague, threw yet another light upon him:

> Freud's simplicity was a familiar characteristic to those who knew him, yet it is something very hard to convey. One tends to think of this great man who produced this immense volume of work in his lifetime, and who was occupied with such totally new, unheard-of, and sometimes obscure ideas, as a completely sophisticated being, surveying the world and the objects of his study from a detached distance. It is quite untrue; behind the dignity and reserve of a serious, much-occupied professional man, he was a most unsophisticated person and sometimes quite naive. (Riviere, 1958: 147)

Freud's reserve is a common thread, which runs through different descriptions. Some would extend that feature to his closest relationships. Roazen, for example, summarizes Freud's family relations as 'tender' but 'remote and perhaps neglectful' and cites as an example Freud's holidays as a time for his writing, and not for his family (1979: 486). Other biographers only partially concur. Clark, for example, quotes Freud's joy at being on holiday in the mountains: 'delightful solitude – mountain, forest, flowers, water, castle, monastery, and not one human being' (1980: 198). It is what we might expect of one who could in places write about humanity with undisguised disdain. On the other hand, Freud shared this joy in his letters to his family; and Freud's children remembered with equal joy the games they had with him on holiday, especially his favourite one of collecting mushrooms.

Roazen also claims that Freud was much more interested in his psychoanalytic family than his natural one, although other biographers provide plenty of examples of the interest he showed in, and pleasure he gained from, his children and grandchildren: 'When our little Mathilde chuckles we think it the most beautiful thing that could happen to us' (Clark, 1980: 112). His son Martin described Freud as 'a gay and generous father' and his daughter Anna echoes this with the words 'even tempered, optimistic and even gay' (Gay, 1989: 158–9). Gay also suggests that Freud was not very demonstrative, and that he was formal and reserved, but more able to express warmth to his daughters than to his sons. Another part of family life were Freud's dogs, which he loved dearly, saying that their advantage over human beings was that he felt towards them no ambivalence and no element of hostility. Indeed, one of his dogs sat in on many sessions with patients, even knowing before Freud did when the analytic hour was completed, yawning to the minute to announce the end of the session! (Clark, 1980: 484).

His even-temperedness is confirmed by a letter his widow Martha wrote to a family friend, referring to the fact that in fifty-three years of marriage not one angry word had fallen between them. It is difficult to know how much she exaggerated in her grief when she wrote this, although no one can doubt her sincerity about how 'terribly difficult it is to do without him. To continue to live without so much kindness and wisdom beside one!' (Clark, 1980: 530). His son Martin also recalled a childhood incident when his father, who could have been very angry, turned what felt for Martin like a 'soul-destroying tragedy' into 'an unpleasant and meaningless trifle' (Gay, 1989: 162).

Yet Freud could also be angry, although references to this only occur in relation to psychoanalytic disputes. He could get very irri-tated, and, once aroused, his anger could endure (Roazen, 1979: 287). Gay observes that Freud quickly felt better when he could verbally express his rage (1989: 195). He could continue to feel bitter to those whom he felt had betrayed or deserted him. Attention has also been drawn in various places to his inherent pessimism. He could get depressed, although he was not generally a depres-sive person. All his biographers refer to his deep grief following the death of members of his family, especially those of his daughter Sophie and her son, Freud's grandson, Heinerle.

Freud is sometimes popularly seen as a dogmatic man. Gay qualifies this: he had a regular routine, but he was not rigid. Momigliano records that he was a stickler for punctuality, and never cancelled sessions unless the circumstances were excep-tional (1987: 382). There were certain essential psychoanalytic 'doctrines' that he furiously defended, but he was always open to other ideas (Gay, 1989: 159). The criticism of Freud's intellectual narrowness is one that I examine in Chapter 4. Whatever his public stance, in Freud's home there was little evidence of authoritarian-ism. Although Freud's son Martin later had difficulties with his father over his work in the psychoanalytic publishing house, he described the Freud household as a liberal one. 'We were never ordered to do this, or not to do that; we were never told not to ask questions. Replies and explanations to all sensible questions were always given by our parents, who treated us as individuals, persons in our own right' (Gay, 1989: 161).

Obviously specific aspects of Freud's personality will stand out for different readers as they did for those who knew him. For myself two contrasting aspects stand out. Firstly there is his humour and sense of irony. Gay describes his conversation as 'a model of lucidity and vigor, abounding in original formulations. His fund of jokes, mainly pointed Jewish stories, and his unsurpassed memory for apt passages from poets and novelists, gave him the incomparable gift of relevant surprise in speech and writing alike' (Gay, 1989: 159). It is never quite clear in some of the anecdotes told of Freud just how one should understand his jokes: they are at one and the same time mischievous (and untrue), realistic (and pointedly true), and yet they also express, often with the lightest of touches, the negative feelings one would expect in one who identified the unconscious hostility often expressed through humour. Freud's humorous hostility is sometimes directed towards others, but is also at his own expense.

Typical of the former is the occasion when Freud was required by the Nazis to sign a statement to say that he had not been ill-treated, before the Gestapo would let him leave Vienna. He signed as he was asked, and added the written comment: 'I can most highly recommend the Gestapo to anyone' – a risky piece of sarcasm, which was apparently not perceived.

Typical of the latter was a time when a pupil praised *The Future of an Illusion*. Freud replied 'This is my worst book! It isn't a book of Freud. … It's the book of an old man! … Besides Freud is dead now, and believe me, the genuine Freud was really a great man. I am particularly sorry for you that you didn't know him better' (Roazen, 1979, 521–2).

But the other feature is one that is described by Bruno Goetz in a short article on three meetings with Freud when Goetz was a student. Freud listened to Goetz, and talked a little about his family. His 'prescription' consisted of some money to buy a decent steak, as well as advice on diet. At the second meeting they discussed Goetz's poetry and Freud's atheism, and Goetz's record, made immediately afterwards, quotes Freud as saying:

> 'What I have been saying to you just now is not at all scientific and it has done me good to play with ideas a bit, instead of continually imposing a strict discipline on myself. The serious business of your life will be in a totally different sphere, and your good conscience will be of a different kind. The main thing is never to lose heart. And never have yourself analysed. Write good poetry, if it is in your power to do so, but don't become shut in on yourself or hide yourself away. One always stands naked before God: that is the only prayer we can still offer.'

> (Goetz, 1975: 142)

The last meeting is not recorded in detail, but concludes: 'When he shook hands with me as I was leaving, he looked straight at me, and once again I felt the tender, sad warmth of his gaze. The memory of that look has remained with me all my life' (Goetz, 1975: 143).

Chapter 3 describes Freud's approach in more detail, mainly through the case studies in which he records his observations: from those and from accounts by some of his patients we can deduce something of his practice as an analyst. It was from his work with patients and his own continuing self-analysis that he derived many of his theories, which I summarize in Chapter 2. But a reading of Freud, as a therapist and as a thinker, should perhaps always be set against Goetz's experience of him: 'As a man, Freud had greater breadth, richness, complexity and – I'm glad to say – more inherent contradictions than his teaching' (Goetz, 1975: 139).

2
Freud's Major Theoretical Contributions

so many long-forgotten objects
revealed by his undiscouraged shining

are returned to us and made precious again;
games we had thought we must drop as we grew up,
little noises we dared not laugh at,
faces we made when no one was looking.

W.H. Auden: 'In Memory of Sigmund Freud'

Four Corner-Stones

Freud's psychoanalytic theory developed continuously for more than forty years. During that time he not only expressed the results of his own thinking, which drew deeply upon his self-analysis and reflecting upon his work with his patients, thereby creating an idiosyncratic set of theories; but he also drew upon ideas suggested by his colleagues. While therefore it is tempting to criticize Freud's work for being too much based upon his personal experiences, it is important to recognize that he read widely, fastidiously acknowledged his sources, and gave space to ideas that he could not whole-heartedly accept – such as Rank's theory of the importance of birth trauma (1933a: 120).

Given so many years' development of his theories, and the wide range of issues which he discussed in what amount to twenty-three volumes in the Standard Edition, it is no easy task to identify the most important of his ideas. Freud himself stressed acceptance of certain key theories as essential to the practice of psychoanalysis, which provides a starting point. An encyclopaedia article by Freud lists the corner-stones of psychoanalytic theory as:

> the assumption that there are unconscious mental processes, the recognition of the theory of resistance and repression, the appreciation of the importance of sexuality and of the Oedipus complex – these constitute the principal subject-matter of psychoanalysis and the foundations of its theory. No one who cannot accept them all should count himself as a psychoanalyst. (1923a: 145)

Elsewhere Freud adds a fourth hypothesis to this list of essentials –
'the importance of infantile experiences' (1925d: 223). These markers
provide a clear path into Freud's theory, although in this chapter I
also summarize other aspects of his theory, which form a speculative metapsychology – attempts to describe the structure of the
mind and the theory of instincts or drives, and the application of
psychoanalytic theory to group psychology, art and literature,
religion and civilization itself. It is nevertheless necessary to
observe at the outset that Freud puts his weight behind these
essential corner-stones, and does not insist on the same kind of
acceptance for his other ideas.

The Unconscious

The concept of unconscious aspects of mental processes was not
Freud's discovery. The nineteenth century with its increasing
study of human nature, and the description of its inwardness seen
in the development of the novel, had long recognized the existence
of unconscious parts of the mind: unconscious motivation, the
unconscious as the source of poetic creation, the links between
the unconscious and dreams. Philosophers like Schopenhauer
and Nietzsche, poets such as Goethe, Schiller, Wordsworth and
Coleridge, novelists such as Charles Dickens, George Eliot and
Henry James, all describe directly or indirectly the importance of
unconscious feelings and thoughts.

What distinguished Freud's contribution is that he gave to the
term 'unconscious' a substantive status, seen in the title of his
longest paper on metapsychology *The Unconscious* (1915e).
Summarizing his thinking to date in the *Introductory Lectures* Freud
writes: '"Unconscious" is no longer the name of what is latent at
the moment; the unconscious is a particular realm of the mind with
its own wishful impulses, its own mode of expression and its
particular mental mechanisms which are not in force elsewhere'
(1916–17: 249). Different phenomena such as hypnotism, dreams,
slips of the tongue and the pen, neurotic symptoms and acts, as
well as irrational behaviour, required the assumption of the unconscious (Gay, 1989: 367). Freud felt that there had to be a place
where what was unacceptable to the conscious mind was
repressed and held, and from which the repressed emerged from
time to time, in one form or another, back into consciousness. In
using such a topographical term as 'place' I seem to suggest, as
Freud might seem to suggest, that it is possible to locate the unconscious in a particular part of the brain. Freud did not intend to give
the topography of the unconscious such a meaning, or at least he

holds his options open: 'our psychical topography has *for the present* nothing to do with anatomy; it has reference not to anatomical localities, but to regions in the mental apparatus, wherever they may be situated in the body' (1915e: 177, Freud's italics).

Freud described the special characteristics of the unconscious. For example, its processes pay little regard to reality; they are not bound by time; they are much more mobile than conscious processes; they can be displaced from one idea to another, or condensed into a form that is capable of expressing many different ideas, as is consciously expressed in the pun. Neither is the unconscious logical, so it can permit contradictions. 'When two wishful impulses whose aims must appear to us incompatible become simultaneously active, the two impulses do not diminish each other or cancel each other out, but combine to form an intermediate aim, a compromise' (1915e: 190). All these characteristics can be seen *par excellence* in dreams.

Freud was nevertheless uncomfortable with the notion of the unconscious put forward in his 1915 paper and in the *Introductory Lectures* (1916–17). He revised his views in *The Ego and the Id* (1923b) and summarized them in the *New Introductory Lectures* (1933a). He comments in the latter that 'at first we are inclined greatly to reduce the value of the criterion of being conscious since it has shown itself so untrustworthy. But we should be doing it an injustice. As may be said of our life, it is not worth much, but it is all we have' (1933a: 102). It is indeed the conscious that provides the illumination with which we can study the depths of the mind.

In his later writing he distinguishes three aspects of the unconscious. There is first that which easily enters consciousness, known as the pre-conscious. A memory can readily be called to mind, sparked off by a trigger word and association of some sort. Say the word 'school' to yourself, and you will recall an incident or series of incidents from school-days, which a minute ago were not in your conscious mind, but now are. The second aspect of the unconscious is more truly unconscious, where accessing memories is very hard, if not impossible. It may require some weeks, months or even years before certain memories can be allowed back into consciousness. This other aspect is where 'transformation is difficult and takes place only subject to a considerable expenditure of effort or possibly never at all' (1933a: 103). Then there is a third aspect to the 'system unconscious', as Freud calls it, 'a mental province rather than a quality of what is mental' (1933a: 104), foreign to the ego. This he called, from 1923 onwards, the 'id' (see 'The Structure of Personality', p. 61).

It needs to be stressed that Freud's attempts to describe the unconscious were bold in the extreme, since by definition the unconscious in his psychology, like the deity in theology, is unseen and unknowable. To suggest that there is an unconscious is one thing: to attempt to outline its workings another. In practical terms the unconscious is best seen at work in its effects, or as Freud put it: 'the path led from symptoms to the unconscious to the life of the instincts, to sexuality' (1933a: 88). It was the cure of symptoms that first drew Freud into exploring the unconscious, as he surmised that feelings and ideas arising from actual events (and later in his thinking also from fantasies) were repressed into the unconscious, and returned as symptoms such as hysterical conversion. In addition to symptoms, dreams, slips of the tongue, etc. and jokes provide glimpses of feelings and ideas repressed in the unconscious. His theories about these formed the basis of his earliest writing, and should therefore be described first before moving to the second of the major corner-stones, repression.

Dreams

Dreaming provides 'our first glimpse of the processes which take place in the unconscious system' (1933a: 46). Dreams are the work of the mind during sleep, where their function is to preserve sleep. They are a way of incorporating external stimuli, such as the alarm clock ringing, which turns in the dream into a bell, or the draught when the bedclothes slip off, which in the dream becomes a snow-storm; and a way of processing internal stimuli (often from the day before, particularly unfinished business, some of which stimuli also reactivate concerns from the past). Where these stimuli can be converted into dream work, sleep can be maintained. 'Dreaming allows the product of a collaboration of this kind to find an outlet in a harmless hallucinatory experience and in that way assures a continuation of sleep' (1933a: 45). The dream that wakes the sleeper is one that has not been successful enough in performing this function.

Every dream contains points of contact with the previous day but may also borrow from childhood. 'The deeper one carries the analysis of a dream, the more often one comes upon the track of experiences in childhood which have played a part among the sources of that dream's latent content' (1900a: 287). The dream is also a wish fulfilment. At first Freud thought that every dream was a wish fulfilment, but later he also distinguished those that recall recent and earlier traumata, although the latter too embody the wish to master the trauma that is still buried in unconscious memory.

Freud's stress on the difficulty of gaining access to what is truly unconscious is apparent in the distinction he made between the manifest content of a dream and its latent thoughts. The manifest content is what the dreamer remembers upon waking, and is what the dream appears to be telling the dreamer. It is often in the form of pictures and symbols. The latent thoughts are words and associations that arise from thinking where the pictures and symbols might take the dreamer in her or his thoughts. Such thinking is known as free association. Freud gives some simple examples of associations pointing to latent thoughts in *The Introductory Lectures*: such as the man who dreamt that his brother was in a box. The word 'box' triggered the thought 'cupboard', and the noun 'cupboard' triggered off an association to a reflexive verb meaning 'restricting himself'. The brother in a box is the manifest content: the brother restricting himself is the latent thought. Obviously more elaborate dreams tend towards more complex associations, especially since dreams employ two other devices, which Freud identified as displacement and condensation.

Displacement means the replacement of latent elements by something more remote, by an allusion that disguises the latent thoughts of the dream, because latent thoughts are subject to dream censorship. The important elements are therefore shifted to unimportant features, and often to apparently senseless and strange images and events, which are what are most often remembered upon waking. Behind the 'strange dream I had last night', therefore, are thoughts that are not so readily permitted into consciousness.

The second feature of the manifest content of the dream as remembered upon waking is that one image may represent a number of ideas, which have been brought together through a process of condensation. As Freud illustrates this, a single person in a dream may be the result of a compilation of several people of your acquaintance: 'A composite figure of this kind may look like A perhaps, but may be dressed like B, may do something that we remember C doing, and at the same time we may know that he is D' (1916–17: 205–6). A number of ideas or thoughts may therefore be hidden behind one symbol, although they may have something in common which binds them together.

There is no better way of testing Freud's theories of dream work than one's own dreams, just as Freud himself described many of his own in his key book *The Interpretation of Dreams*. In one of his recorded dreams he had written a monograph on an unspecified plant. This 'botanical monograph' arose from impressions the previous day, when Freud had seen a monograph on cyclamens in a bookshop. His associations 'led by numerous connecting paths deeper and deeper into the tangle of dream-thoughts' (1900a: 387).

The word 'botanical' was related to a Professor Gardener, the blooming looks of his wife, a patient called Flora and a story of forgotten flowers, which then led to his wife's favourite flowers, to an episode at school and to an examination at university. These thoughts were not simply isolated associations to the word 'botanical'. They had all occurred in a conversation with Dr Konigstein, the colleague with whom Freud had shared his discovery of the anaesthetic qualities of cocaine, which Freud had written up in a monograph. He traces similar associations from the word 'monograph'. Freud concludes: 'This first investigation leads us to conclude that the elements "botanical" and "monograph" found their way into the content of the dream because they possessed copious contacts with the majority of the dream-thoughts ... and because they had several meanings in connection with the interpretation of the dream' (1900a: 388).

In his major study of dreams Freud wrote that 'the interpretation of dreams is the royal road to a knowledge of the unconscious activities of the mind' (1900a: 769). Nevertheless it is important to note that such detailed analysis of dreams as appears in that book is more suited to the scientific study of dreams than to dream work in psychoanalytic therapy in more recent years (see Chapter 3). Freud himself later lamented the loss of interest in the dream in psychoanalytic circles (1933a: 36); and it has been noted how few attempts there have been to revise Freud's dream theory in the light of his own development of the structure of personality (Brennen, 1993: 51–2). Furthermore, later research into dreams has indicated that the manifest content may be more important than Freud allowed for, and later analytic interpretations of Freud's key 'Irma dream' have indeed dwelt on the significance of its manifest content (Flanders, 1993: 9).

Slips and Jokes

Although dreams contain many examples of the unconscious mind at work during sleep, it is in slips of the pen and the tongue, and other types of what Freud termed 'faulty functions' of the mind, that we see how unconscious processes equally slip through to consciousness – in waking life. Bettelheim has observed that the Standard Edition translation of Freud's phrase 'faulty function' – parapraxis – completely fails to express the ordinariness of these examples from daily life: 'a term such as "parapraxis" interferes with a true appreciation of what Freud called the psychopathology of everyday life' (1983: 88). The book of that title is one of Freud's most popular and accessible works (1901b/2002), which uses very ordinary language. (For a useful discussion of the problems of translating Freud when so many of the original translators' terms have become psychoanalytic jargon, but far from capable of being fully understood by the ordinary reader, see the introduction to the 2002 translation (Freud 1901b/2002: xxxv-xl, xliv-xlviii).

Freud provides many examples of the way in which thoughts that are pushed back – consciously suppressed or unconsciously repressed – slip out again through the mistakenly spoken or written word, through forgetting, in losing objects, or in bungled actions. Examples of 'faulty functions' demonstrate occasions when the mind is not successful in maintaining its suppression or repression of words and actions that are thought likely to be censored, either by others or by oneself. In the book on everyday life and in his first three *Introductory Lectures* Freud provides many examples of faulty functions. One simple illustrative occasion occurred on holiday when he met two Viennese women walking in the Dolomites. They discussed together the pleasures and trials of a walking holiday. One of the women admitted that it was not pleasant tramping all day in the sun and perspiring through one's blouse and chemise. She appeared to hesitate in mid-sentence, as it turned out obviously avoiding continuing with her catalogue of clothes, but in the next sentence she said that 'when one gets "nach Hose" and can change ...', Freud was too polite to point out to her that she had substituted the word *Hose* ('pants'), which she appeared to have censored when she paused in the previous sentence, for the similarly sounding and intended word *Hause* (home).

There was to Freud's mind also a resemblance between dreaming and the origin of jokes: 'a preconscious train of thought is abandoned for a moment to be worked over in the unconscious, and from this it emerges as a joke' (1916–17: 274). Jokes also appear in dreams, although with little of the pleasure of a true joke. Similarly, jokes condense various thoughts, two or more of which may stem from the same word, such as a pun. Other jokes keep the listener in suspense, then release the listener's pleasure through laughter by means of the punch line, a phenomenon which had some resemblance to the tension and release present in sexual pleasure.

Repression

Of all Freud's theories, repression was perhaps the most important. He certainly singled it out as a special corner-stone 'on which the whole structure of psychoanalysis rests. It is the most essential part of it; and yet it is nothing but a theoretical formulation of the same phenomenon which may be observed as often as one pleases if one undertakes an analysis' (1914d: 73). In other words, in the consulting room evidence of repression was seen every time there were signs of resistance.

The term 'repression' had been used earlier by the philosopher Schopenhauer in 1844, although Freud said that he did not read his work until much later in life. The term also appears in the writings of the psychologist Herbart in 1824, whose work influenced one of Freud's teachers, and may therefore have indirectly influenced Freud. He first used the expression in an initial publication written with Breuer, which was later to form the first chapter of their *Studies on Hysteria* (1895d). They used the term to describe a phenomenon whereby feelings that are unacceptable are repressed from conscious thought. As a concept it helped to explain the origin of the symptoms of hysterical conversion. These resulted from an initial situation in which a patient's feelings were excited, but were experienced (before even emerging into consciousness) as unacceptable to the 'dominant mass of ideas constituting the ego' (1895d: 180–1). The ideas and feelings were held back in the unconscious by the force of repression. However, the idea was not always successfully held back, and so found its way to expression indirectly and 'all the more easily along the wrong path to a somatic innervation' (1895d: 180).

Such a concept employs a mechanistic quasi-hydraulic image: feelings and ideas are dammed up, but under growing pressure find an alternative way to flow into consciousness. This is known as 'the return of the repressed'. The further away from the original excitation is the alternative expression of it, the more likely it is to be allowed into consciousness. Repression takes highly individual forms, and it is exceedingly mobile. It is also continuous and requires the expenditure of considerable energy: 'the process of repression is not to be regarded as an event which takes place *once*, the results of which are permanent, as when some living thing has been killed and from that time onwards is dead; repression demands a persistent expenditure of force, and if this were to cease, the success of the repression would be jeopardized, so that a fresh act of repression would be necessary' (1915d: 151). Freud cites as an example how an animal phobia may be the displaced result of love for the father, repressed due to fear of father, emerging as fear of a wolf; although Freud admitted that in such a brief description he did not 'supply an adequate explanation of even the simplest case of psychoneurosis: there are always other considerations to be taken into account' (1915d: 155). Indeed, it is not always clear why repression should be necessary, except through fear or because of pain. The closest Freud gets to a reason for repression is the need to avoid 'unpleasure'. Neither is the relationship between repression and anxiety clear, since in one place Freud describes repression as creating anxiety, although in earlier writing he says that it is anxiety that creates repression.

In his 1915 paper on the subject, Freud uses the term 'repression' to describe every type of blocking of ideas and feelings, and appears to equate it with the generic term 'defence'. In his later work he uses different terms to distinguish forms of defences, of which repression is the most important: in earlier papers these forms are just *examples* of repression, not separately identifiable defences. For instance, in the paper on *Repression* (1915d) Freud uses the term 'displacement' as an illustration of repression, but later this is identified as one of the defences in its own right. Other forms of defence serve the same purpose as repression, of keeping conscious awareness at a distance from forbidden or feared feelings or ideas. However, these other defences employ different methods of achieving this. Among the defences which Freud identifies is the familiar term 'projection': 'an internal perception is suppressed, and, by way of substitute, its content, having undergone a degree of distortion, is consciously registered as an external perception' (1911c/2002: 56). In fact Freud only refers to this type of defence once in connection with paranoia, and in persecutory delusions he believes that a further transformation takes place, in which feelings of love are turned into feelings of hate.

Three of the forms of defences are particularly associated with obsessional symptoms. Reaction formation, although in large part less successful as a defence, describes the replacement of negative feelings (such as sadism) with their opposite (such as compassion). 'Undoing' is a kind of 'negative magic' (Gay, 1989: 488–9), seen in the example of the Rat Man's deepest sympathy whenever anyone died (Freud, 1909d/2002: 189), which Freud saw as a way of trying to undo the death wishes the patient had towards his father. 'Isolation' describes a defence in which shameful or painful emotions (or affects) are detached from certain memories, which are recalled only in an unemotional way.

In a late paper on *Fetishism* Freud distinguishes further between repression as applying to the distancing of feelings, and 'denial' as the distancing or 'disavowal' of an idea; he mentions it in the context of a boy or man observing that a woman does not have a penis, but having to deny such a perception altogether by asserting that she has – which the man takes to be present in the form of the fetish that excites him (1927e: 352–3).

Sublimation

There is just one form of redirecting psychological energy towards a different object and a different aim that Freud sees as being quite different from repression or other defences. This is where feelings, particularly sexual feelings, can be inhibited in relation to their original object, or given expression in a different aim than direct discharge on the one hand, and repression and subsequent neurosis on the other. Such energies can be (and indeed have been) channelled into art and literature, into scientific discovery and the pursuit of knowledge, and into the formation of civilization itself. 'The manner in which the sexual instincts can thus be influenced and diverted enables them to be employed for cultural activities of every kind to which indeed they bring the most important contributions' (1925d: 222). Freud observes that homosexuals in particular have demonstrated this capacity for sublimation. He is less sure whether women show that capacity, at least in relation to culture and the formation of civilization; but Freud, as I will make clear, often sees women as lacking in much more than a penis: his estimation of their psychological abilities suggests they are generally inferior to men.

Indeed, if Freud attaches great importance to the way in which sexual energies had and have been both inhibited in their aim and rechannelled into the development of culture and civilization, he provides other examples of sublimation which are clearly just as, if not more, applicable to women. He cites, as another example of sublimation, the capacity for tenderness, 'which undoubtedly originates from the sources of sexual need and invariably renounces its satisfaction' (1933a: 129). Nevertheless, sublimation has similar fragility and, like repression and defences, it can revert to its original aim when the energies channelled into sublimation become over-strong, and break through. Freud gives as an example the breakdown of civilization: since it is built, in his view, largely on the suppression of sexual instincts or drives, under pressure the instinctual forces can break through, unleashing hostility and aggression and lawlessness (see 'Society, Religion and Culture', p. 64). Similarly, on the level of family relationships, if we take the second example of sublimation that Freud gives, that of tenderness, it is possible to understand that such an appropriate expression of sexual love between a parent and a child can also break down under pressure. Although the object (the child) remains the same, the feeling reverts to its original aim, corrupting tenderness into sexual abuse.

Instincts or Drives

This discussion of sublimation has introduced various technical terms, which are central to Freud's theory, and which need clarification if sexuality, the Oedipus complex and the importance of infantile experience are to be more fully understood. Such clarification is all the more important since this aspect of Freud's theory changed more than any other over the forty-five years of his published work. What starts out as virtually a biological/mechanical theory, ends with major hints (though no more than that) of object relations theory: and this is perhaps the single most important development of post-Freudian theory.

Freud's wish for a scientific basis for psychoanalysis pushed him, especially in his early years, into a materialistic model. Indeed, as late as *The Ego and the Id* (1923b) and *The New Introductory Lectures* (1933a), Freud uses two (different) diagrams of the mind, as if he wishes to create a physical representation of the personality (see 'The Structure of Personality', p. 61), although he makes it clear that 'we cannot do justice to the characteristics of the mind by linear outlines like those in the drawing' (1933a: 112).

Some of his critics within psychoanalysis (for example, Guntrip, 1971; Schafer, 1976) believe psychoanalysis to be an interpretative discipline, and have questioned whether 'a psychology predicated on mechanically defined drives, and on structures derived from the transformation of drive energy, can adequately fulfil this psychoanalytic goal' (Greenberg and Mitchell, 1983: 22). Greenberg and Mitchell themselves observe that people interpret experience in many different ways, looking for meaning. Freud drew upon biological metaphors, which is what one would expect of a 'theorist trained in medicine in the intellectual climate of late-nineteenth-century Vienna' (1983: 23). He was undoubtedly influenced by eminent scientific thinkers such as Helmholtz and Brücke. Yet Freud was later to point to the metaphorical or mythical quality of his instinct theory, which 'is so to say our mythology. Instincts are mythical entities, magnificent in their indefiniteness. In our work we cannot for a moment disregard them, yet we are never sure that we are seeing them clearly' (1933a: 127).

It is important to recognize that 'instinct theory', the term most commonly used in English translations, is in Freud's original text a theory about drives. The translators mistranslated *Trieb* (they said for reasons of style and grammar) as 'instinct' rather than 'drive', although Freud himself seldom used the word 'instinct', except when referring to lower animals. *Trieb* describes a feeling of being driven, or an impulse, but a persistent rather than a momentary one (see Freud 1930a/2002: xxvi–xxvii). The principal drive/impulse Freud identified was a sexual one, libido or (in later references) Eros. Freud commented in the 1920 Preface to *Three Essays on Sexuality* that 'anyone who looks down with contempt upon psychoanalysis from a superior vantage-point should remember how closely the enlarged sexuality of psychoanalysis coincides with the Eros of the divine Plato' (1905d: 43).

Greenberg and Mitchell distinguish three distinct phases in the development of Freud's drive theory, the first before the publication of *Three Essays on Sexuality* in 1905, the second between 1905 and 1910, and the final phase remaining largely unaltered after 1910. (It was the structural model of personality which particularly developed in this last phase.) In the first phase Freud gave weight to the 'constancy principle', where the greatest pleasure came from a sense of quiescence or constancy. Any rise in excitation of libido resulted in tension, and the aim of the organism was to keep tension low. Sexual tensions therefore had to be discharged, and if not directly, other means were necessary. Two forms of neurosis arose when discharge was not possible: firstly, actual neuroses, so defined because they were caused by current problems in a person's sexual life, and *physiological* in origin since 'sexual substances' could not be discharged; and *secondly* psycho-neuroses, *psychological* in origin, 'brought about by the incompatibility of ideas and the consequent failure to discharge affect [feeling]' (Greenberg and Mitchell, 1983: 27). The most likely content of these conflicting ideas was considered to be sexuality. It is not surprising that in those early years of practice, great emphasis was placed upon catharsis, or the discharge of blocked memories together with their associated feelings and ideas.

It is this particular version of drive theory that has provoked the greatest criticism, such as by Guntrip, who rejects the idea that sexuality can be compared to a drive or impulse like hunger, or defecation: 'In a sexual relationship both increase and diminution of tension and excitation are pleasurable if and when they are phases of a total satisfying relationship. Excitation becomes unpleasant only when the relationship is interfered with and left incomplete' (Guntrip, 1961: 128). Indeed, in the second phase of his drive theory Freud distinguished different drives, those which were ego-preserving, such as hunger, and those which were object-seeking. He also distinguished between libido or love directed towards oneself (narcissism) and that which was directed towards other people and the world (object-love).

The second phase of Freud's drive theory was more fully developed, since he recognized the need for a specific source of excitation. Freud saw most of a child's early experience of libidinal drives as auto-erotic: obtaining satisfaction from one's own body, a 'happily chosen term introduced by Havelock Ellis' (1905d: 97). If the child experiences libidinal excitation, there must have been some early experience that had given a 'taste' of this (my phrase, not Freud's), which in turn links to the full expression of sexual satisfaction in adult life:

> It is clear that the behaviour of a child who indulges in thumb-sucking is determined by a search for some pleasure which has already been experienced and is now remembered. ... It is also easy to guess the occasions on which the child had his first experiences of the pleasure which he is now striving to renew. It was the child's first and most vital activity, his sucking at his mother's breast, or at substitutes for it, that must have familiarized him with this pleasure. ... No one who has seen a baby sinking back satiated from the breast and falling asleep with flushed cheeks and a blissful smile can escape reflection that this picture persists as a prototype of the expression of sexual satisfaction in later life. (1905d: 97–8)

We notice here that the object of the drive is now as important as the drive itself: auto-eroticism is a substitute for the breast, and the breast is in one way 'the prototype of every relation of love' (1905d: 145). It is equally possible to see adult sexual experience as an attempt to recapture that earliest experience: 'The finding of an object is in fact refinding it' (1905d: 145). So in the third phase of Freud's drive theory 'much of his work was devoted to integrating relational concepts into the established structure of the drive model' (Greenberg and Mitchell, 1983: 25).

Other drives to which Freud alludes include the drive for knowledge and the drive for mastery. The most controversial aspect of his drive theory is that of the death instinct, or death drive (Thanatos), which he first put forward speculatively in 1920. Bettelheim comments that the mistranslation of *Trieb* as 'instinct' did great harm to the idea of the death drive (1983: 106). In fact 'Freud never spoke of a death instinct – only of a mostly unconscious drive or impulse that provokes us to aggressive, destructive and self-destructive actions (1983: 107). It was partially an explanation of masochism, but it was deeper than that.

As Bettelheim more convincingly explains it:

> For Freud, the I was a sphere of tragic conflict. From the moment we are born until the moment we die, Eros and Thanatos struggle for dominance in shaping our lives, and make it difficult for us to be at peace with ourselves for anything but short periods. ... It is this struggle which makes emotional richness possible; which explains the multifarious nature of a man's life; which makes alike for depression and elation; which gives life its deepest meaning. (1983: 109)

Few of Freud's followers felt able to take up this particular theory (including many who, at that time, would not have been put off, as Bettelheim suggests non-German speakers have been, by the later mistranslation). Bettelheim makes out a convincing case for recognizing the reality of death, and that there is a sense in which we are driven (or dragged) towards death throughout life. Yet Freud also uses the death drive as a way of explaining the origin of aggression, and in his hypothesis was perhaps over influenced by his own potentially terminal illness and by the nihilistic pessimism and angst of mid-European philosophers such as Nietzsche. Freud made an essential attempt to integrate aggression into his theory, but his explanation was a less than satisfactory outcome for what remains a complex subject.

Sexuality: Aims and Objects

Freud's book *Three Essays on the Theory of Sexuality* was first published in 1905, but he added to and revised his thinking with every edition. The present version, last revised in 1920, therefore represents a record of Freud's developing theory. As will become clear below, where I summarize the second and third of the *Three Essays*, further revisions concerning both the development of personality and gender issues appeared in subsequent publications. It is the first of the essays that is particularly relevant since it introduces and distinguishes sexual aims and sexual objects.

The importance of this essay is that it provides a transitional position between Freud's earliest drive-based theory and his later position, which is itself a preliminary statement of what is known as object relations theory. Object relations theory lies at the centre of most modern psychoanalytic thinking. It stresses personal relations rather than drives. In drive theory other people are important inasmuch as they either assist or frustrate me in the satisfaction of my most significant drives; in object relations theory drives are important inasmuch as they enable me to achieve the aim of making and sustaining relationships with significant others. There is actually more to object relations theory than this, such as in the development of Freud's theory of the structure of personality. It is not only external relationships with objects that become more important in his later theory: we also have the first hint of the importance of internalized relationships and objects within the personality (see 'The Structure of Personality', p. 61).

The first of the essays on sexuality launches straight into two technical terms: 'sexual object' and 'sexual aim'. The sexual object is the person towards whom sexual desires are felt (and often expressed). While the term object seems impersonal, it is used primarily in the sense of the 'object' of an active verb (I [subject] like him [object]); but it incidentally conveys the sense in which the object can also be either itself impersonal, or a person treated impersonally. In this essay Freud questions the universality of the supposedly normal sexual object, an adult person of the opposite sex. He examines first, but without any prejudice, a major deviation from the norm, the 'invert' or homosexual. That Freud did not regard homosexuality as psychologically abnormal, and certainly not as a neurosis, may come as a surprise to those who are aware of the way in which psychiatry and psychoanalysis psycho-pathologized homosexuality for the greater part of the twentieth century. It is refreshing to read, in every reference Freud makes in this essay and elsewhere to homosexuality, that far from it being neurotic, it is part of normal development, and an aspect of every person's sexuality. Freud's emphasis on bisexuality in personal development may have got him into difficulties when he came to examine the psychology of women, but in the matter of homosexuality it served to help him integrate this type of sexual object choice. Freud observes that inversion is found in people who show no other signs of deviation from the normal, in people whose efficiency is unimpaired, and 'who are indeed distinguished by specially high intellectual development and ethical culture' (1905d: 49).

That is not to say he is uninterested in the explanation of homosexuality, but here again his breadth of judgement means that he sees various possibilities in object choice and gender identification, some constitutional, some the result of cultural and societal norms, and some to do with relationships to mother and father in infancy. 'We are not in a position to base a satisfactory explanation of the origin of inversion upon the material at present before us' (1905d: 59).

Freud concludes this section with a reference to truly psychopathological instances of sexual object: those who choose sexually immature persons or animals as objects. It is important to note that here Freud asserts (as he continued to do throughout his life) the incidence of actual sexual abuse. Some of the fiercest criticism of Freud suggests that he withdrew his theory of actual sexual seduction altogether. Time and again this can be shown to be an ignorant accusation. Here, for example, he asserts that 'sexual abuse of children is found with uncanny frequency among school teachers and child attendants, simply because they have the best opportunity for it' (1905d: 60).

The sexual object is the object of a person's sexual feeling. The sexual aim is the means of expressing sexuality. 'The normal sexual aim is regarded as being the union of the genitals in the act known as copulation, which leads to the release of the sexual tension and a temporary extinction of the sexual instinct' (1905d: 61). In this part of the essay Freud is again more interested in deviations from the normal, which he calls perversions. Perversions are defined as aims which either '*extend*, in an anatomical sense, beyond the regions of the body that are designed for sexual union or … *linger* over the intermediate relations to the sexual object which should normally be traversed rapidly on the path towards the final sexual aim' (1905d: 62, Freud's italics).

In the former category Freud includes various extensions: over-valuation of the sexual object, so that the desired object becomes the supreme authority; oral and anal sex (normally inhibited, he suggests, by what he regards as somewhat irrational disgust); and fetishism. Fetishism is the inordinate desire for a single part of the body, such as hair or feet, although Freud recognizes a certain degree of such desire as present in normal expressions of love. In the idea of such extensions, Freud appears to describe, without being yet able to give it the technical term used in later object relations theory, the 'part-object', where one single part of a person (especially of the body) is a forerunner of the whole person (as in the case of the breast), or becomes a substitute for the whole person. What distinguishes fetishism is that the sexual aim does not pass beyond such parts of the body, and takes the place of the normal aim.

The second category of perversion, lingering over or fixation, includes supplanting the sexual aim with looking and being looked at: in neurotic form known as voyeurism, and its antithesis, exhibitionism. Freud also refers to excessive aggression (of which a certain amount is, he feels, present in the normal sexual act): he here adopts terms which a Viennese expert in nervous diseases, Krafft-Ebing, had coined – sadism and its counterpart masochism. It is important to notice that throughout this essay, Freud describes as deviations the exaggerated significance given to *normal* aspects of sexuality: 'if, in short, a perversion has the characteristics of *exclusiveness* and *fixation* – then we shall usually be justified in regarding it as a pathological symptom' (1905d: 75, Freud's italics).

The connection of perversion to neurosis forms the final part of the first essay on sexuality. Neurotic symptoms arise not only 'at the cost of the so-called *normal* sexual instinct ... but they also give expression (by conversion) to instincts which would be described as *perverse* in the widest sense of the word if they could be expressed directly in phantasy and action without being diverted from consciousness' (1905d: 80, Freud's italics). Instead of being expressed (and here Freud gives a clear example of the use of a hydraulic model) 'the libido behaves like a stream whose main bed has become blocked. It proceeds to fill up collateral channels' (1905d: 85). Neuroses are what Freud calls 'the negative', but which we might call 'the alternative' expression of perversions. Furthermore, as the first essay concludes, 'a formula begins to take shape which lays it down that the sexuality of neurotics has remained in, or been brought back to, an infantile state' (1905d: 87).

Freud's Theory of Development

To write frankly about sexuality in 1905 was not unique. Freud was able to draw upon the example and thinking of such authors as Krafft-Ebing and Havelock Ellis. The bolder step was to repeat in print the ideas that had drawn such fierce criticism ten years before, the theory of infantile sexuality. Freud's theory of personal development is now so familiar that it is difficult to envisage the impact it first made. At this distance what was a controversial theory seems unduly limited, with its inadequate attention to gender differences, with its over-emphasis on the physical and under-emphasis on personal relations, and with its comparative neglect of the mother in the whole process. As a model of human development it fails to give adequate consideration to adult life with its own developmental sequence: it was Erikson who provided such an extended model fifty years later (1950). Nevertheless, in breaking such new ground, as well as in the validity of many of its observations, Freud's model was a major achievement. 'So far as I know, not a single author has clearly recognized the regular existence of a sexual instinct in childhood; and in the writings that have become so numerous on the development of children, the chapter on "Sexual Development" is as a rule omitted' (1905d: 88–9). He was later to find only one forerunner, G. Stanley Hall, who had published one year before him in America.

Freud identified three early stages of sexual development, followed by a period called 'latency'. A second phase of development started at puberty. Thus, sexual development was 'diphasic', in two major phases. Originally the early stages were confined to what are familiarly now known as the oral, anal and genital stages, although later Freud added a third pre-genital stage, known as the phallic stage, leaving full genital development until puberty. Between the phallic and the genital stages there occurs what Freud was later to name the Oedipus complex. In order to make his theory clearer, I devote a separate section to a fuller explanation of the Oedipus complex (see p. 54); and following that I discuss the more vexatious question of Freud's psychology of female development (p. 57).

'The sexual aim of the infantile instinct consists in obtaining satisfaction by means of an appropriate stimulation of the erotogenic zone which has been selected in one way or another' (1905d: 101). Freud's theory is based upon a sequence of such erotogenic zones, starting with the mouth, moving to the anus, and finally to the genitals. The sexual object is in the main the child's own body: one of the main characteristics of infantile sexual life is its auto-erotism. Freud appears to neglect the child's relationship with parents, although, as we have already seen, he suggests that the auto-erotic is in itself an attempt to recapture the experience of being at the mother's breast. (Later psychodynamic theory would see the breast as a 'part-object', one part of what the adult knows as a whole object, the mother.)

The first stage (Freud's term is 'sexual organization') is the oral or cannibalistic stage, where sexual activity has not yet been separated from feeding. 'The *object* of both activities is the same; the sexual *aim* consists of the *incorporation* of the object – the prototype of a process which, in the form of *identification*, is later to play such an important psychological part' (1905d: 117, Freud's italics). The principle of incorporation and identification indeed plays an important part in the development of object relations theory, as becomes clearer when I examine Freud's theory of the formation of the super-ego (see 'The Structure of Personality', p. 61).

The second pre-genital stage involves a 'sadistic-anal' organization, which includes an active principle, 'the instinct for mastery through the agency of the somatic musculature' (1905d: 117), together with a passive principle, the erotogenic zone of the anus. Although the emphasis here appears to be upon defecation and micturition, Freud made it clear that it appears that there is sexual pleasure in muscular activity generally: 'we are all familiar with the fact that children feel a need for a large amount of muscular exercise and derive extraordinary pleasure from satisfying it. Whether this pleasure has any connection with sexuality ... is open to critical questioning' (1905d: 122). Freud also drew attention to the ability of the child to use excretory functions not simply auto-erotically, but in the way they relate to adults. 'The contents of the bowels have other important meanings for the infant. They are clearly treated as a part of the infant's own body and represent his first "gift": by producing them he can express his active compliance with his environment and by withholding them, his disobedience' (1905d: 103–4).

In the *Three Essays on Sexuality* Freud followed the anal with the genital stage of organization. The genitals now become the focus of pleasure – although they have already been stimulated in the washing and rubbing of bathing in earlier life. This observation led Freud eventually to speculate whether the mother was the first person 'unavoidably' to arouse the child sexually, and so implant fantasies of 'seduction', which later became attached to the father as the sexual seducer in infancy (1931b: 386).

In his later theory Freud added a 'phallic' stage to his description of sexual development, although this is already implicit in *The Three Essays*, where he refers to the two riddles that children try to resolve: the origin of babies, and genital differences. Boys, he said, assume that all human beings have the same male form of genitals. They deny vehemently that girls are different, and 'recognize the female clitoris as a true substitute for the penis' (1905d: 114). (It is worth considering this sentence as a statement of Freud's own difficulty too, when he came to formulate his psychology of female development.) Girls do not have to resort to this kind of denial, recognizing boys' genitals as formed differently from their own. Instead, they 'are overcome by envy for the penis – an envy culminating in the wish ... to be boys themselves' (1905d: 114).

In a short essay written in 1923 Freud expresses his dissatisfaction with the primacy of the genitals in infancy. 'What is present is not a primacy of the genitals, but a primacy of the *phallus*' (1923e: 308, Freud's italics). He honestly admits that he is describing the male child: 'the corresponding processes in the little girl are not known to us' (1923e: 309). The phrase is a good example of his modesty, which in other places gives way to a certain dogmatism. Boys move from thinking that the girl's clitoris is an even smaller penis than their own, to 'the emotionally significant conclusion that after all the penis had at least been there before and had been taken away afterwards' (1923e: 310), and they fear castration. Loss or threatened loss of the penis is not the first 'narcissistic injury through a bodily loss': the experience of losing mother's breast in weaning, and 'the daily surrender of his faeces' and 'even his separation from the womb at birth' (1923e: 310n) are also types of castration. Note here the importance of symbolic language, which must always be considered as what Freud and other analysts mean in statements that might otherwise be taken too literally by the reader.

What is significant about the phallic stage is that at this point in infantile genital organization, *'maleness* exists, but not femaleness. The antithesis here is between having a *male genital* and being *castrated*. It is not until development has reached its completion at puberty that the sexual polarity coincides with *male* and *female'* (1923e: 312, Freud's italics). Such a formulation was an interim position, carried through into Freud's later writing on female sexuality (see 'Gender and Female Psychology', p. 57) where the lack of a penis and the inferiority of the clitoris continue to feature. However, in his last papers, unlike this paper on the phallic stage, where development of both genders is related to the norm of male sexuality, Freud shifted his ground again. Although he appears in places to hold to identical development in boys and girls in the pregenital stages (1933a: 151), he made a significant recognition of the way girls and boys differ in their earliest relationships, for example pre-Oedipal exclusive attachment to mothers is greater in women than men (1931b: 377).

In Freud's earlier theory genital organization is reached in childhood; in his later theory it is in adolescence. Between the two phases there is a period known as latency, lasting 'from about the sixth to the eighth year' to the onset of puberty in which 'we can observe a halt and retrogression in sexual development' (1916–17: 368). Although Freud said that this period was culturally determined, 'a product of education', he also felt that this development 'is organically determined and fixed by heredity' (1905d: 93). In his later work Freud saw latency as ushered in by resolution of the Oedipus complex (see p. 54), at least for boys, although for girls it is more like a continuation, since for girls the Oedipus complex 'is not destroyed, but created, by the influence of castration' (1931b: 376). Although the latency period appears somewhat sterile emotionally (and for that reason is open to question in the form Freud gave it), he observed that 'all through the period of latency children learn to feel for other people who help them in their helplessness and satisfy their needs a love which is on the model of, and a continuation of their relation as sucklings to their nursing mother' (1905d: 145). Thus, latency seems an important transitional stage on the way towards the formation of loving relationships in adolescence.

'The Transformation of Puberty' is the title of the third of *The Three Essays*. The sexual drive, which until now has been largely auto-erotic, now seeks a sexual object outside itself. There are two ways of finding an object. The first is the 'anaclitic', based upon attachment to early infantile prototypes, meaning, for example, finding a partner reminiscent of mother or father. Freud explicitly related the finding of an object at the end of latency to the restoration of the original relationship to the mother's breast (1905d: 144). The second form of object choice is 'narcissistic', which means in this instance seeking one's own ego by finding it again in other people (1905d: 145n).

Adolescence also sees the formation of 'sentimental friendships with others of their own sex' (1905d: 153); and a 'detachment from parental authority, a process that alone makes possible the opposition, which is so important for the progress of civilization, between the new generation and the old' (1905d: 150). Freud observes that young girls are less able to separate, persisting in their 'childish love far beyond puberty' (1905d: 150), partly because of 'an exaggerated need for affection and an equally exaggerated horror of the real demand made by sexual life' (1905d: 151). However, in a paper a few years later Freud acknowledges a more important and relevant brake on the development of young women. Society has a double standard, so that young men are able to express their sexuality, whereas young women have their sexuality suppressed:

> It is clear that education does not take lightly the task of suppressing a girl's sensuality until she marries, for it operates with the harshest means. Not only does it forbid sexual intercourse and put a high premium on the preservation of female innocence: it also shields the young woman from temptation as she matures, by keeping her in ignorance of any factual knowledge about the role she is destined for and by refusing to tolerate any amorous impulse that cannot lead to marriage. (1908d/2002: 99)

This is of course a statement that needs to be taken in historical context: it would be far less true today, although some of the sentiments about double standards are surely often just as true? Freud was equally realistic about the psychological health of women in marriage. Looking beyond adolescence he painted a pessimistic picture of adult sexual relationships. Men 'quite often avail themselves of whatever freedom they are allowed, though only tacitly and reluctantly by even the strictest sexual code' (1908d/2002: 796). It is women who suffer most. As early as 1892 Freud suggested that 'neurasthenia in women is a direct consequence of neurasthenia in men' (cited by Young-Bruehl, 1990: 4); and later that 'when afflicted by marital disappointments, [women] fall prey to severe neuroses, which permanently darken their lives'. Indeed, 'a girl has to be fairly healthy in order to "cope" with marriage' (1908d/2002: 97). Freud's conclusions about marriage are bleak indeed: 'In this state of mental disappointment and physical deprivation, which is thus the fate of most marriages, both partners find themselves back in the state they were in before they married, except they are now bereft of an illusion' (1908d/2002: 96). Perhaps that is why, with the exception of his theory of the sublimation of sexuality through art, literature and science, Freud paid little attention to psychological development in adulthood. It is almost as if we spend our adult life living out the conflicts of childhood and adolescence.

The Oedipus Complex

Freud did not use the phrase 'Oedipus complex' until the mid period of his writing (1910h: 238). He had two years before used the term 'nuclear complex' and had referred to the Oedipus myth and theme in *The Interpretation of Dreams* (1900a: 356–66). The very first reference is found in his correspondence with Fliess:

> Being totally honest with oneself is a good exercise. A single idea of general value dawned on me. I have found, in my own case too, [the phenomenon of] being in love with my mother and jealous of my father, and I now consider it a universal event in early childhood. ... If this is so, we can understand the gripping power of *Oedipus Rex* ... the Greek legend seizes upon a compulsion which everyone recognizes because he senses its existence within himself. Everyone in the audience was once a budding Oedipus in fantasy and each recoils in horror from the dream fulfillment here transplanted into reality. (Masson, 1985: letter dated 15 October 1897)

This is followed through in *The Interpretation of Dreams*, where Freud examines the affections of children for the parent of the opposite sex. He observes how men tend to spoil their daughters and women their sons, and he cites sayings of children such as 'Mummy can go away now. Then Daddy must marry me and I'll be his wife' (1900a: 359). Thus, 'being in love with the one parent and hating the other are among the essential constituents of the stock of psychical impulses which is formed at that time' (1900a: 362). This he felt to be confirmed by the legend of Oedipus, which is worth summarizing here:

   As a baby, Oedipus was left to die by his father Laius, because an oracle warned Laius that his son would be his murderer. The child was rescued and grew up in another city, not realizing he was the adopted son of his new parents. As a young man Oedipus learned that he should avoid his home since he was destined to murder his father and marry his mother. Oedipus therefore left the place he believed to be home, but met Laius (his natural father) on the road, and slew him in a quarrel. Then, by solving the riddle of the sphinx, he released Thebes (his birthplace) from the creature's power. He married Jocasta (the widow of Laius, and his natural mother although of course not known to him) as a reward. When a plague broke out, once more threatening Thebes, Oedipus set about finding its cause: who had murdered the king?

> The action of the play consists of nothing other than the process of revealing, with cunning delays and ever-mounting excitement – a process than can be likened to the work of a psychoanalysis – that Oedipus himself is the murderer of Laius, but further that he is the son of the murdered man and of Jocasta. (1900a: 363)

When he found out the truth, Oedipus blinded himself and once more left Thebes.

As Freud describes it, Oedipus is

> a tragedy of destiny. Its tragic effect is said to lie in the contrast between the supreme will of the gods and the vain attempts of mankind to escape the evil that threatens them … It is the fate of all of us, perhaps, to direct our first sexual impulse towards our mother and our first hatred and our first murderous wish against our father. Our dreams convince us that this is so. (1900a: 363–4)

Jocasta too, in the original drama by Sophocles, says 'many a man ere now in dreams hath lain with her who bare him' (quoted by Freud, 1900a: 366).

Bettelheim has argued that Freud would have understood the myth to be about the *wish to avoid* incest and parricide: a wish so strong that Laius and Jocasta left their baby child to be killed, and later led Oedipus to leave his (adoptive) home. What happened, says Bettelheim, resulted (in psychological terms) from Oedipus' early traumatization in being rejected by his natural parents. Bettelheim agrees with Freud about the strength of the Oedipal feelings that have been repressed from childhood, and about adults being unconsciously motivated by and unconsciously guilty about such feelings. When the repressed hostility and long-ings can be made accessible, they cease to have such damaging consequences (Bettelheim, 1983: 22).

The tragic consequences in the myth can be repeated in the Oedipus complex when parents break the taboo on incest, and re-enact the Oedipal story. The early credence that Freud gave to stories of actual seduction (normally of girls by fathers) gave way in his thinking to the explanation that neurosis is more frequently caused by fantasies of seduction and other repressed sexual fantasies. Freud did not completely retract his belief in actual seduc-tion, despite what a number of important critics have suggested. I return to these arguments in Chapter 4. What needs stressing here is that when there is actual sexual abuse, or even emotional seduction of children, or the use of children by parents as allies in their own warring relationship, this makes the possibility of resolution of the Oedipus complex much more difficult. 'Where seduction intervenes it invariably disturbs the natural course of the developmental processes, and it often leaves behind extensive and lasting consequences', wrote Freud towards the end of his life – clearly again not a retraction (1931b: 379). Freud's insight into the significance of Oedipal relationships remains central to his theory in whatever way it may be acted out in families.

The Oedipus complex was indeed for Freud 'the central phenomenon of the sexual period of early childhood' (1924d: 315). Despite its possible tragic consequences, for most children it 'is bound to pass away according to programme when the next pre-ordained phase of development sets in' (1924d: 315). This it does, Freud believed, because the male child comes to fear castration – a fate that he imagines women have already suffered, since they lack a penis. The child fears castration as a mark of disapproval for early masturbation (including bed-wetting, which is seen as a form of genital pleasure). The child also fears retaliation by the father for the child's wish to replace the mother; although at the same time the boy child also wishes to replace mother in father's eyes, and to be loved by him. Given the choice of love for his parents at the cost of his penis, the child opts for 'his narcissistic interest' (1924d: 318), the protection of part of his body, and turns away from the Oedipus complex. The objects he desired and feared are given up and replaced by identifications, which form the nucleus of the super-ego. This explanation of the creation of the super-ego was another important step towards internalized object relations, and is examined further below (see 'The Structure of Personality', p. 61).

The Oedipus complex is 'a metaphor operating on many levels' (Bettelheim, 1983: 21). It clearly refers to three-person relationships, particularly within the family, although the three persons involved are not only mother, father and child. Siblings may also be involved, but since Freud linked the metaphor of castration to the earlier loss of the breast and the giving up of faeces, this suggests that a 'third force' may also be the weaning mother coming between the child and the breast, or the parent countermanding the child's wish to retain her or his faeces. The feelings of love and hate towards the parents generated in such situations resemble the ambivalent feelings towards them in the more regular version of the Oedipus complex. When, as in much else in Freudian theory, his concepts are given this status of metaphor, it is possible to see just how frequently this concept might appear, in different guises, in psychodynamic therapy. Some of the criticisms of Freud's ideas are more aptly directed towards his translators, who in putting together the Standard Edition in English resorted to neologisms in order to try and clarify Freud's ideas. In doing so they lost sight of the way 'Freud used ordinary-language metaphors to express many of his technical concepts' including some of the most central ones (Cheshire and Thomä, 1991: 451).

Gender and Female Psychology

Freud wrote a vast amount about sexuality, but this must not be confused with gender. Most of what I have examined above relates either to children regardless of gender, or more specifically to boys. In *The Dissolution of the Oedipus Complex* Freud made it clear that he was more confident writing about male children. In attempting to describe the corresponding development in girls, the 'material – for some incomprehensible reason – becomes far more obscure and full of gaps' (Freud, 1924d: 320).

Freud later gave as his reason for this that as a male analyst he was provided with less transference evidence than his female colleagues (1931b: 373). Roith cites evidence to show that Freud denied both the extent of the influence of Judaism on him and also the importance of his mother. She suggests that his theories of women are linked both to his Jewish origins, and to his unwillingness to confront issues around his relationship with his mother, although he also idealized the mother–son relationship as 'altogether the most perfect, the most free from ambivalence of all human relationships' (Freud, 1933a: 168). His views of women were also influenced by Judaism: 'the Jewish woman never achieves an autonomous adult state, so that she must defer to a man on any question of religious observance' (Roith, 1987: 122–3).

For all his shortcomings, when it came to the psychological development of girls and women Freud was not content to accept his initial theory of a common developmental path for children of both genders.

> The insight that the existence of personality differences between the sexes required an explanation was a major intellectual leap, and it is Freud who must be credited with that insight. Thus, psychoanalysis was the first comprehensive personality theory that attempted to explain the origins of what we now call gender. (Person and Ovesey, 1983: 203)

The Oedipus complex is a simpler process for a girl than for a boy; but it is not, it is important to note, the Electra complex. This was Jung's term, and one which Freud rejected on the grounds that it 'seeks to emphasize the analogy between the attitude of the two sexes' (1931b: 375). In his earlier theory Freud believed that just as a boy was attached to his mother (in his pre-genital organization as well as in the Oedipus complex), so a girl was similarly attached more to her father than her mother. This seems to have added very little to his theory at that point in time.

In Freud's later theory the situation is different: a girl's earliest relationships are recognized as being focused on her mother. 'The phase of exclusive attachment to the mother, which may be called the *pre-Oedipus* phase, possesses a far greater importance in women than it can have in men. Many phenomena of female sexual life which were not properly understood before can be fully explained by reference to this phase' (1931b: 377, Freud's italics). One example Freud cited was that women choose husbands who then inherit the bad aspects of their wives' relationships with their mothers. When it comes to the Oedipus complex there are some similarities, but 'it seldom goes beyond taking her mother's place and the adopting of a feminine attitude towards her father' (1924d: 321). This begins to happen when the girl realizes that she does not possess the same genitals as the boy. In a series of dramatic sentences Freud describes his view of her reactions to this discovery: 'She makes her judgement and her decision in a flash. She has seen it and knows that she is without it and wants to have it. ... After a woman has become aware of the wound to her narcissism, she develops, like a scar, a sense of inferiority' (1925j: 336, 337). The girl blames her mother 'who sent her into the world insufficiently equipped' (1925j: 338). But this anatomical deficiency is not the only reason for reproach. There is a second 'rather surprising one. It is that her mother did not give her enough milk, did not suckle her long enough' (1931b: 381).

There is in fact little evidence that mothers suckle baby girls less than boys, but Freud appears (inadvertently?) to have used an image that has received some support from feminist psychoanalytic studies. Chodorow notes the difference between her assessment of the researchers of academic psychologists (who say there is little differential treatment of girls and boys) and the reports from psychoanalysts of 'increasing evidence of distinction between the mother's basic attitudes and handling of her boy and girl children starting from the earliest days' (1978: 99). If we take insufficient milk as another metaphor, it appears that it is more often women who can feel 'empty of oneself' (1978: 100). Chodorow suggests that while 'most women do develop a sense of separate self' (1978: 110), this is more of a struggle for them, since this is not something that their mother gives them as definitively as she does her sons. 'Separation and individuation remain particularly female developmental issues' (1978: 110).

As a result of her disillusionment with her mother, a girl 'gives up her wish for a penis and puts in place of it a wish for a child: and *with that purpose in view* she takes her father as love-object' (1925j: 340, Freud's italics). There is, however, a crucial difference: whereas in boys it is their love for mother which pushes them into the Oedipus complex, and their fear of castration and their identification with father that ushers them out of it, girls enter the Oedipal situation by virtue of their castration complex, but never really work through the Oedipus complex in the same way as boys.

According to Freud, the super-ego in women is therefore less well developed: 'they show less sense of justice than men ... they are less ready to submit to the great exigencies of life ... they are more often influenced in their judgements by feelings of affection or hostility' (1925j: 342). Although this may seem a patronizing statement, a few lines before this Freud says that women's 'super-ego is never so inexorable, so impersonal, so independent of its emotional origins as we require it to be in men' (1925j: 342). Freud's perception here is that women and men make moral decisions in a different way, but he gives no actual indication (apart from citing popular opinion) that women's moral judgement is *inferior* to men's. Here again Freud unknowingly anticipates later research, particularly that by Carol Gilligan, who argues that men and women have different conceptions of morality, men focusing on issues of justice, fairness, rules and rights, whereas women emphasize people's wants, needs, interests and aspirations (Gilligan, 1982).

If there are differences between women and men (and Freud rejects what he sees as the attempts of feminists to blur differences), Freud also challenges the assumption that there are character differences between men and women based upon such terms as 'active' and 'passive'. He argues (1933a: 147–9) that psychologically there need be no difference between men and women – to call men active and women passive has no real basis other than social convention; 'we must beware in this of underestimating the influence of social customs, which ... force women into passive situations' (1933a: 149). Indeed, he seriously questions whether it is possible to label a woman as being passive at all, when she is so clearly 'active in every sense towards her child' (1933a: 148). The description is only true inasmuch as the male sex-cell is active and mobile and seeks out the passive female sex-cell. In every other respect, Freud argues, these terms are inaccurately imposed by society. The further one moves from the sexual sphere the more inaccurate what he calls this 'error of superimposition' (the equivalent of stereotyping) becomes. 'Women can display great activity in various directions, men are not able to live in company with their own kind unless they develop a large amount of passive adaptability' (1933a: 148). He is aware too that men disparage women because it is men who regard women as being castrated (1931b: 376). It is not such a far step from there to say that castration anxiety is more of a problem for men, than it is for the majority of women.

Brief though his essays on gender differences are, Freud places more emphasis on pre-Oedipal factors in a girl's development than he does in writing about boys. He admits that his study of pre-Oedipal phases in boys is incomplete, and 'it is probably more prudent in general to admit that we have as yet no clear understanding of these processes, with which we have only just become acquainted' (1931b: 383). This is a startling admission to make for one who as early as 1905 had published his essay on the three phases of infantile sexuality, two of which were pre-Oedipal. It was perhaps his desire to defend the ground of sexuality and the Oedipus complex, as well as his difficulty as a man (and as his mother's son) in acknowledging the powerful position of a mother, that prevented him from looking more deeply into these matters earlier.

In his essay on *Female Sexuality* there are hints of what Freud might have developed had he been a younger man, with his earlier energy for following through his questioning: for example, that boys have a difficult transition to make, from identification with mother to identification with father. Previously the assumption had been (and indeed it was repeated in these essays) that it is girls who have the more difficult move to make, from mother as their love-object to father as love-object. For boys, mother is their first and the natural model, making it perhaps less easy than he had hitherto thought for boys to achieve masculinity than it might be for girls to achieve a feminine identity. Perhaps, as some feminist psychoanalysts have suggested, men achieve masculinity in a more extreme form as a reaction against their wish to identify with the mother (Dinnerstein, 1987). As I demonstrate in Chapters 4 and 5, it probably required the feminist therapists to make clear the significant differences between mother–boy and mother–girl relationships; and to highlight the differing contributions made to gender development by individual nurturing and child-rearing, and by the power structures within society.

The Structure of Personality

At this juncture this review of Freud's theories turns towards aspects that are inherently even more hypothetical than anything described so far. Some of Freud's theories may have been distorted, partial or wrong, but many were attempts to explain the direct observations that he made in his self-analysis and the analysis of his patients. In the theories that follow we enter territory that is much more speculative: hence it is known as metapsychology, 'beyond psychology', since it attempts to describe the unobservable. This is also true of Freud's excursions into sociological and anthropological disciplines.

It may come as a surprise that the familiar terms 'ego', 'id' and 'super-ego' appeared late in Freud's writing (when he was well over 65 years of age); and also that these terms, which appear so technical, in the original German were attempts to communicate in a commonplace way. Freud used the ordinary pronouns 'I', 'It' and 'Over-I', and (as indicated already) it was his English translators who insisted on turning them into quasi-scientific latinate forms. Bettelheim comments:

> Freud's careful and original choice of words facilitated an intuitive understanding of his meaning. No word has greater and more intimate connotations than the pronoun 'I'. ... If anything, the German *Ich* is invested with stronger and deeper personal meaning than the English 'I' ... Where Freud selected a word that, used in daily parlance, makes us feel vibrantly alive, the translators present us with a term from a dead language that reeks of erudition precisely when it should emanate vitality. (Bettelheim, 1983: 53–5)

James Strachey, who was the translator of the Standard Edition, partly followed Ernest Jones's advice, since Jones wished to create an 'international standard' in areas where there were uncertainties and ambiguities in Freud's work (see Ornston, 1992). The term 'Id', for example, is substituted for the German *das Es*, which in common parlance simply means 'It', as in 'It just came over me.' This term was one which Freud borrowed from a rather wild analyst, Georg Groddeck, who may in turn have taken it from Nietzsche, who used the term for the impersonal in human nature. The 'id' is 'the dark, inaccessible part of our personality; what little we know of it we have learnt from our study of dream-work and the construction of neurotic symptoms, and most of that is of a negative character and can be described only as a contrast to the ego ... we call it a chaos, a cauldron full of seething excitations' (1933a: 105–6). It is filled with energy reaching it from the instincts (i.e. drives), but it has no organization, and strives to satisfy instinctual needs subject to the observance of the pleasure principle: the achievement of pleasure and the avoidance of tension or unpleasure. The id is full of contradiction; it is timeless; and it has no moral sense. It is in these latter respects like the unconscious, although the unconscious also contains part of the ego and super-ego as well.

Freud used the term 'ego' as far back as *Studies on Hysteria*, where he borrowed the phrase 'primary ego' from Janet and his followers (Freud and Breuer, 1895d: 153). The ego there seems to serve the principal function of warding off unacceptable ideas (1895d: 180). In later theory the ego is turned towards the external world, and 'is the sense-organ of the entire apparatus ... receptive not only to excitations from outside but also to those arising from the interior of the mind' (1933a: 107–8). Freud believed that the ego is partially formed from part of the id, but modified by the need to relate to and react to the external world. It borrows its energies from the id. The ego is concerned with 'reality-testing' (1933a: 108). Unlike the id, the ego synthesizes and tries to combine and unify its mental processes, producing a high degree of organization. It

> develops from perceiving the instincts to controlling them. ... To adopt a popular mode of speaking we might say that the ego stands for reason and good sense, while the id stands for the untamed passions. ... The ego's relation to the id might be compared with that of a rider to his horse. (1933a: 109)

What is never clear in Freud is whether the ego is, as it seems to be described above, one aspect of the personality, or whether it is to be equated with 'the self'.

The concept of the 'super-ego' or 'Over-I' is of particular interest, over and above any part it plays in Freud's structural map of the mind, since it prefigures much object relations theory. The origins of the super-ego (or as Freud also calls it, the ego ideal) lie in the resolution of the Oedipus complex, where the child identifies with father or mother: certain aspects of parental injunctions come to occupy a permanent place within the child's mind. The ego ideal is seen in the 'precept: "*you ought* to be like this (like your father)". It also comprises the prohibition: "You *may not be* like this (like your father)"' (1923b: 374, Freud's italics).

Freud identifies an important parallel to the formation of the super-ego in the process of mourning. He did not appreciate when he wrote his paper on *Mourning and Melancholia* (1917e) how common and typical such a process was: 'since then we have come to understand that this kind of substitution has a great share in determining the form taken by the ego and that it makes an essential contribution towards building up what is called the "character"' (1923b: 367–8). When the external object is lost, it is replaced within the personality by a representation of the same object taken inside the ego (technically known as the 'introjected' object): 'an object which was lost has been set up again inside the ego – that is an object-cathexis [investment] has been replaced by an identification' (1923b: 367).

This process, variously known as internalization, identification or introjection, was most important for the later development of Freudian theory, since through it Freud gave active expression to 'internalized objects'. These are representations of aspects of relationships, once lost or given up, and since incorporated into a person's 'inner world'. Parents (mother and father, in their good and bad aspects) continue to operate within the personality even when they are not physically present. While Freud only suggested one internal object, the super-ego, he opened up the possibility of other internalized objects or part-objects, such as Klein's theory of the internalized good breast and bad breast, living on within the personality, influencing inner world reactions and relations as much as outer world relationships. (For a fuller description of these processes see Wallis and Poulton, 2001: chap. 2)

In Freud's structural theory it is the ego that has to mediate between internal and external pressures. It 'serves three severe masters ... the external world, the super-ego and the id' (1933a: 110). Freud's description of the demands on the ego are vivid and sympathetic, ending with the cry: 'Life is not easy' (1933a: 110–11). In its most precise form Freud summed up his structural theory with the phrase 'an action by the ego is as it should be if it satisfies simultaneously the demands of the id, of the super-ego and of reality – that is to say, if it is able to reconcile their demands with one another' (1940a: 377–8). When this happens the reality principle triumphs against the pleasure principle (1911b: 40–1).

When this attempt to mediate breaks down, neurosis is a common outcome. Neurosis occurs when 'people turn away from reality because they find it unbearable – either the whole or parts of it' (1911b: 35). Freud described psychosis as an extreme form of turning away from reality, and he held out little hope of psychoanalysis being of value in such instances. He believed that various aspects of culture assisted the task of replacing the pleasure principle with the reality principle. Religion does so, but through renunciation of pleasure, thereby not conquering the pleasure principle. Science comes close to replacing the pleasure principle, and is able to offer displaced intellectual pleasure in the process. Education helps the developmental process and assists the ego. It is interesting that it is art, above all, that brings about a 'reconciliation between the two principles' (1911b: 41). An artist turns away from reality, and 'allows his erotic and ambitious wishes full play in the life of phantasy' but comes back to reality 'making use of his special gifts to mould his phantasies into truths of a new kind, which are valued ... as precious reflections of reality' (1911b: 41–2).

Society, Religion and Culture

In his latter years Freud's energies and enthusiasm extended into many other disciplines. It was a result of his wish that psychoanalysis should extend its horizons, but it was also an indication of his ever-questioning mind that he could apply himself to literature, to art, to anthropology, to religion and to sociology; and that he could propose answers to questions about the existence of God, the dynamics of large groups, the nature of civilization, as well as the psychology of artists such as Leonardo da Vinci, Michelangelo and various literary figures. He is most often here expressing personal opinions, without the backing of the experimental situation that he was afforded in his work with patients. But he encouraged the interplay of psychoanalysis with a number of other disciplines, a forerunner for the application of psychoanalytic ideas to literature, sociology, film, etc. – areas I discuss further in Chapter 5.

The problem of being an individual and also being a member of wider society was raised in a major study by Freud called *Civilization and Its Discontents* (1930a/2002). Civilization, Freud suggests, has required the suppression of instinctual needs; it has also brought advantages, since society protects and provides. Nevertheless, this is at a cost, which inevitably also produces discontents, such as the inhibition of sexuality and aggression.

In an earlier book, which touched on the same subject, *Group Psychology and the Analysis of the Ego* (1921c), Freud uses two examples of organizations, the church and the army. In it he draws upon Le Bon's crowd psychology and Trotter's herd instinct. Freud suggests that what binds people together in a large group is their internalization of their leader, Christ or the general, and their identification with each other. In choosing to belong to the church, for example, individual members give up some of their own ego to the ego ideal of Christ. They are held together by love for Christ, and by the belief that Christ loves all the members of the church equally; but, Freud asks, what happens to the hostility which has been suppressed in order to maintain this loving institution?

One way in which this is expressed is towards people outside the religious group. Freud writes that even if the church is held together by bonds of love, it may be hostile and cruel to people outside it. Christianity 'even if it calls itself the religion of love, must be hard and unloving to those who do not belong to it' (1921c: 128). He thinks this is also true of other faiths. Every religion is 'a religion of love for all those whom it embraces; while cruelty and intolerance towards those who do not belong to it are natural to every religion' (1921c: 128).

Freud's analysis of religion appears in other shorter works (for example, 1907b, 1933a: Lecture 35), as well as in major works such as *Totem and Taboo* (1912–13), where he translates the Oedipus myth into an anthropological setting, believing that in the primal horde a band of brothers had conspired to kill, consume and then idealize the dominant male; *The Future of an Illusion* (1927c), 'an essentially negative valuation of religion' (1925d: 257); and *Moses and Monotheism* (1939a), perhaps the most eccentric and unfortunate book he ever wrote, which came close to offending his Jewish supporters, and which made an even stronger attack on Christianity for its anti-Semitism. Freud sees religion as a universal obsessional neurosis, although he also equates neurosis with a 'private religion' (1907b: 33). He describes the function of religion in this way: 'it gives [human beings] information about the origin and coming into existence of the universe, it assures them of its protection and of ultimate happiness in the ups and downs of life, and it directs their thoughts and actions by precepts which it lays down with its whole authority' (1933a: 196–7). (See also on this subject Jacobs, 2000.)

Freud's profound observation in this connection was that God is a projection of the parent figure. In this he was not original, but he provided a psychological explanation for what had already been similarly suggested by the positivist philosopher Comte, as well as Voltaire, Diderot, Feuerbach and Darwin. Freud was also strongly influenced by the physiologist Brücke, who had supervised him for six years, and who had an aversion to all mysterious explanations drawn from nature.

One of Freud's biographers, Peter Gay, in an earlier book looking at the relevance of Freud's Jewish background to his theory, asserts that 'Freud's identification with Judaism was aggressively secular' (Gay, 1987: 124). He concludes that the search for 'a Jewish intellectual ancestry' is not productive (1987: 129). Freud's intellectual debts were to German and English culture, philosophers, poets or scientists, although Gay also suggests that Freud's Jewishness was 'an indefinable elusive element at work in him' (1987: 132).

It is important to take a step back from the immense theoretical canvas upon which Freud painted to remember its beginnings, with his observation of both his mentors at work and his patients in the presentation of their symptoms. It is easy to forget that the clinical lay at the heart of all his work, and that as he tried to make sense of his observations he inevitably produced a theory which was stronger in some aspects than in others, but which was continuously open to development. With the increasing acceptance of his ideas, Freud turned his attention to these broader issues, extrapolating from the particular to the universal; from the individual to society; and from individual origins to the history of the human race (or as it is sometimes termed, from the ontogenetic to the phylogenetic).

Essentially, theoretical concepts 'provide the invisible backdrop, the unseen framework, within which the analyst hears the patient's story. Thus, basic concepts within psychoanalytic theory provide interpretative possibilities for orientating the clinician towards crucial and hidden dimensions of meaning by informing his sensibilities as a listener' (Greenberg and Mitchell, 1983: 15–16). It is easy to forget that for Freud the situation was different. He had little to go on other than what his patients told him, his self-analysis, what he observed and surmised, and his brilliant imaginative capacity. With the legacy of such an abundance of ideas and publications, it is also easy to forget that from the beginning, and throughout most of his life, Freud's working hours were dominated by analytic sessions with his patients. If the practice of most therapists is informed by their theoretical position, Freud's theoretical position was principally informed by his practice. If he is remembered more often for technical ideas, many of which now have assumed a common use within the English language, at heart what he gave us was a special type of research method and a practical technique. To put theory before practice as I have done here may therefore have been to put the cart before the horse. It is to Freud's psychoanalytic practice that our attention is now inexorably drawn.

3

Freud's Major Contributions to Practice

[He] showed us what evil is, not, as we thought,
deeds that must be punished, but our lack of faith,
our dishonest mood of denial,
the concupiscence of the oppressor

W.H. Auden: 'In Memory of Sigmund Freud'

Freud and Psychoanalytic Practice

Many therapists and counsellors whose practice is not psycho
analytic are critical of Freudian technique, on the grounds that it is
cold and impersonal, that through interpretation it presumes to
know answers, and indeed on the grounds that therapy employs
techniques at all. Such broad generalizations are unhelpful, since
psychodynamic therapists are not clones; they differ as people, and
therefore they also differ in the way they relate in therapy, as well
as in the way they choose to apply basic principles of technique. Yet
the non-analytic criticism has some basis in reality. I seek to show
in this chapter that the fault lies not so much with Freud, as with
psychoanalysis, both in its institutionalized form (for which it must
bear some responsibility), and in its mythical form (for which it
cannot). The combination of the two has created a powerful series
of images of Freudian practice, represented on the one hand in
cartoons where the analyst's couch and his banal interpretations
provide the punchline; and on the other in the more severe criticism
that comes from patients (for example, Dinnage, 1989) and therapists (Lomas, 1987). The impression given of Freud's own technique is inaccurate if these later psychoanalytic caricatures are
accepted as correct examples of what he himself developed and
taught. In fact, Freud's early work with patients (I use this title
since it was the term Freud used) led to the development of basic
techniques and attitudes that are now in common use in most talking therapies. It is worth saying again, as I have earlier, that it is
important to read Freud in the original, or at least in translation.
The new translations of many of Freud's most important works,

published from 2002 onwards in the Penguin Classics series, make reading Freud even more straightforward. A much fuller and more complex picture of Freud and his practice emerges from reading his case histories and his papers on technique, than is possible to gain from extrapolating back to his work from later developments.

Study of his papers on technical aspects, most of them written in the period 1911–16, also provides valuable evidence about Freud's practice (see the volume entitled *Wild Analysis* (2002) in the new translations in Penguin Classics). At times in those papers he lays down clearer recommendations than we see him elsewhere observing himself. There are clear examples, recorded in his case histories, and in the memoirs of some of his patients, of Freud's personal style being far less opaque than some of the recommendations he makes for beginners would suggest. Contrariwise, some of his guidelines contain useful advice that is not always so evident in his own accounts of his therapeutic style, such as his warning about telling patients what their symptoms mean instead of waiting for insight to emerge from them. Freud's confidence and position later on in his practice sometimes led him to depend overmuch upon his personal authority. The early Freud was a therapist who learned nearly all of his technique through experiment, through mistakes, through reflecting on his patients' reactions, and in some recorded instances by following up outcome. His later technical recommendations, made partly in response to instances in some of his followers of 'wild analysis' (1910k/2002), or in others of potentially risky experiment (for example, Ferenczi's more active involvement with patients (Dupont, 1995), combine summaries of the better aspects of Freud's approach, as well as the seeds for later hardening of attitudes.

Early Techniques

Freud's earliest experiments involved hypnosis, as well as massage, both of which he used initially in an attempt to relieve his patients of their immediate symptoms, as well as with the further aim (particularly in the case of hypnosis) of encouraging them to explore the origins of their symptoms. Here he describes such a technique with a patient with the pseudonym Emmy von N.:

> Even while I am massaging her, my influence has already begun to affect her; she grows quieter and clearer in the head, and even without questioning under hypnosis can discover the cause of her ill-humour on that day. Nor is her conversation during the massage so aimless as would appear. On the contrary, it contains a fairly complete reproduction of her

memories and new impressions which have affected her since our last talk, and it often leads on, in a quite unexpected way, to pathogenic reminiscences of which she unburdens herself without being asked to. (Freud and Breuer, 1895d: 112)

Freud's approach was acquired partly through observation of Charcot, but also influenced by his senior colleague Breuer and by Bernheim, a doctor in Nancy who also used hypnosis. As a method of relief and cure it had some similarities to the therapeutic model in physical medicine or surgery. Freud relaxed (in some sense anaesthetized) the patient through hypnosis, and then used the hypnotic state and direct questions to the patient to create openings for the exploration of what had caused the initial distress as well as what caused continuing pain. The 'talking cure' was initially a cathartic process – a parallel process psychologically (and viewed historically just as crude) to purging the bowels or blood-letting, common forms of treatment at that time. By using such techniques, often within the comfortable surroundings of a residential nursing home where the patient would also be physically cared for, Freud was able to achieve temporary relief of some of his patients' symptoms. However, he had doubts about how permanent this relief was.

For a number of reasons, as Freud records in his autobiography, he gave up hypnotism and altered his technique of catharsis. He recognized, as Bernheim also did, that 'when the subject awoke from the state of somnambulism, he seemed to have lost all memory of what had happened while he was in that state' (1925d: 211). Bernheim had found that by laying his hands upon the patient's forehead the forgotten memories would usually return. As Freud described it, by assurances and encouragement and perhaps with the touch of his hand he found he could force 'forgotten facts and connections into consciousness' (1925d: 211). It was a more difficult method than hypnosis, but more instructive for the patient. Such a change also recognized the patient as being more than a passive recipient of treatment. The patient's conscious knowledge of what had happened to him in the past, as well as his experience of the relationship within the treatment setting itself, was a necessary part of the process.

Another reason for giving up hypnosis, which Freud listed as a primary one, was that 'even the most brilliant results were liable to be suddenly wiped away if my personal relation with the patient became disturbed' (1925d: 210). With these words Freud describes the glimpse that he first caught of the phenomenon he was to call 'transference' in *Studies on Hysteria* as early as 1895 (p. 390). I devote a section later in this chapter (see p. 86) to Freud's developing understanding of this particular feature of the therapeutic relationship. Freud did not recognize the full significance of this phenomenon in those early years, but what Freud saw even at that point was that 'the personal emotional relation between doctor and patient was after all stronger than the whole cathartic process' (1925d: 210).

Only the sofa (Freud did not use the term 'couch') remained as evidence of this early period of experiment: Freud abandoned hypnosis, but still wished to encourage the state of relaxation and the dream-like consciousness that had been such an important feature of the hypnotic state: this ambience encouraged the patient to talk more freely. His approach changed to one of asking questions, using where necessary the 'pressure technique', that is pressing his hand on the patient's forehead. This commanding method already shows Freud as an authoritative figure, almost challenging answers to come out of the darkness of unconsciousness. It was an authority that was to have both positive and negative features as psychoanalytic therapy developed.

Surprisingly, given his early recognition of the power of resistance, Freud seemed to get the answers he asked for. The earliest case-studies frequently use phrases such as 'I questioned her', indicating just how active his approach was at this time, although on one occasion the patient called Emmy von N. objected:

> I took an opportunity of asking her, too, why she had gastric pains and what they came from. ... Her answer, which she gave rather grudgingly, was that she did not know. I requested her to remember by tomorrow. She then said in a definitely grumbling tone that I was not to keep asking her where this and that came from, but to let her tell me what she had to say. I fell in with this. (Freud and Breuer, 1895d: 119–20)

There is a similar occurrence in the same case history, where Freud records that he 'saw that I had gained nothing by this interruption and that I cannot evade listening to her stories in every detail to the very end' (1895d: 118). Both references show how Freud's technique was being influenced by his patients. It was gradually to change direction, away from asking questions, to encouraging patients to speak about what they chose. These are perhaps the first ever references to what Carl Rogers much later was to champion as a client-centred or person-centred approach.

Nevertheless, in his technique Freud took this apparently person-centred approach one step further. By laying down just one clear rule to his patients, the rule later known as free association, he added a dimension which person-centred therapy does not specifically include, and which the more active therapies hardly allow. It was not just that Freud encouraged the patient to choose what he or she wanted to speak about, although this was part of his wish: 'you should let the patient tell you something and allow him the choice of where to start' (1913c/2002: 55). Freud extended this simple (and somewhat optimistic) recommendation, when he added that there was an exception to this rule that must be imparted to the patient from the very start. Summed up, it might be described as a request to the patient not simply to choose what to talk about, but to let *everything* that comes to mind be spoken about. The rule of free association required the patient to listen to her- or himself: nothing that came into consciousness should be ignored or omitted. Freud asked his patients to speak about what came to mind without censorship, not making any choice about whether to express one thing rather than another. Person-centred therapists may be encouraged to listen attentively to their clients: but Freud's patients were encouraged to listen attentively to themselves and to everything going on within themselves; and to communicate all this to the therapist.

Later, in this particular paper on technique, Freud summarized this central aspect, describing the fundamental rule, and we might imagine that it was in similar vein that he communicated it to his patient at the start of therapy:

> Just one thing, before you start. Your narrative should be different in one respect from ordinary conversation. Quite rightly, you would normally try to hang on to the threads which hold your account together, and avoid being distracted by intrusive notions and irelevant thoughts, so that you don't get carried away, as they say. But here you are meant to proceed differently. You will notice that during your narrative a number of thoughts will occur to you, which you would like to reject because of certain critical objections. You will be tempted to say that this does not fit in here, or it's completely unimportant, or it's pointless, therefore you don't need to say it. Don't give in to this criticism but say it anyway, precisely because you are averse to doing so ... So you should say everything that comes into your head. Behave like a traveller, for example, sitting in the window seat of a railway carriage and describing to a companion with an inside seat the changing view he is seeing. (1913c/2002: 55–6)

Freud realized that this rule was not one that could be readily adhered to. Some patients would speak very freely, as if they welcomed the permission to speak. Others 'transgress against it from the very beginning' (1913c/2002: 63n).

Encountering Resistance

When Freud moved away from his initial techniques, he saw himself as 'set free from hypnotism' (1925d: 212). That method, which had revealed so much about the potentiality in uncovering the histories of individual patients, had in fact obscured from him more profound observations on the interplay of forces in the human mind. Just as 'repression' was one of the corner-stones of Freud's theory, so its manifestation in clinical practice in the form of the patient's 'resistance' became one of the corner-stones of his developing technique. He asked: 'How had it come about that the patients had forgotten so many of the facts of their external and internal lives but could nevertheless recollect them if a particular technique [such as hypnosis] was applied?' (1925d: 212). Why did patients find it difficult to keep to the rule of free association, so that the way they spoke scarcely seemed 'free'? Freud concluded that 'everything that had been forgotten had in some way been either alarming or painful or shameful by the standards of the subject's personality' (1925d: 212). He felt as if the therapist had to fight against some opposing force within the patient.

The recognition of resistance was a major breakthrough in the development of his therapeutic method. Analysis became a technique primarily aimed at uncovering the presence of resistance, so that the patient could then begin to overcome it him- or herself; and through overcoming it discover the feelings or thoughts that appeared to be resisted. It was uncovering resistance that Freud called 'the art of interpretation' (1925d: 224). Later, interpretation came to include the interpretation of transference as well, because transference was seen as another form of resistance, albeit like other resistance a clue to hidden thoughts and feelings, and likewise present in the way a patient related to the therapist. Freudian interpretation as it is commonly understood tends to mean the linking of past experiences to present feelings and attitudes, but Freud made a clear distinction between 'interpretations' and 'constructions'. The latter term better describes the tentative linking of past and present, through an attempt to reconstruct what may have happened in the past. 'Interpretation applies to an idea, a mistake, etc., some single element of the material, that you are working on. But a construction means that you present the analysand with a part of his forgotten early life-story' (1937d/2002: 215).

The term 'construction' is therefore reserved for that aspect of the therapist's work that follows the process of 'analysis' of resistances (and of the transference). Freud spoke with one of his patients, Elisabeth von R., of his comparison of analysis with an archaeological excavation (see below, p. 76); similarly, 'construction' resembles the reconstruction that the archaeologist makes of an ancient building once most of the buried material has been uncovered (1937d/2002: 213). A construction is therefore more complex than an interpretation. And although it is often thought that Freud emphasized a single traumatic event as the cause of later psychological difficulties, he realized, again in these early years of his psychological practice, that 'as a rule the symptom was not the precipitate of a single such "traumatic" scene, but the result of a summation of a number of similar situations' (1925d: 203).

In the next section, I summarize the case history of Elisabeth von R., treating it at some length since it is one of the clearest examples of Freud's developing technique, both in the way he understood and interpreted resistance, and in the way he made constructions; in this case Freud presents a somewhat over-ambitious construction towards the conclusion of the analysis, in the sense that it might have been difficult to take in even if it were all correct. In addition to Freud's four cases in *Studies on Hysteria* (Freud and Breuer, 1895d), he published a further six case histories in detail, although one of them was the analysis of an autobiography rather than of an actual patient (1911c/2002; see also 1909b/2002; 1909d/2002; 1918b/2002). He also referred to many other patients in shorter illustrations and examples, both in his case histories and in his other theoretical papers. One of the advantages of the Elisabeth von R. case history is that it includes more evidence of his actual practice than later case histories, which tend to concentrate more on the psycho-pathology of the patient.

Freud felt that in some respects the value of case histories was limited, since he had to withhold information to preserve the anonymity of his patients. He noted that it was often the everyday details that he had to disguise: 'one may for more readily divulge to the public a patient's most intimate secrets, since he will then remain unrecognized, than the most harmless and banal features that distinguish his personality, as in this he is known to everyone and will thereby be rendered recognizable to all (1909d/2002: 126). He also recognized that writing notes later made them less accurate than they would have been had he written them during the session. He always wrote his notes the same day and adhered 'as for as possible to what I can recall the actual words used by the patient' (1909d/2002: 172n). He warned against making notes in the session: 'the damage done to the patient by the distraction of the doctor's attention is greater than can be excused by any gain with regard to faithfulness of reproduction in the case history' (1909d/2002: 172n). In any event, Freud believed that 'your selection of the material while you write notes or shorthand will inevitably be harmful to the analysis, and you tie up a part of your thinking capacity that would be better employed in interpreting what you have heard' (1912e/2002: 35). He advised instead that the therapist 'should listen, and not worry whether you notice anything or not' since anything that is 'still disconnected and inchoate, at first appears deeply buried, but readily springs to mind as soon as the patient produces something that connects with it and can develop' (1912e/2002: 34).

In another reference to any value to be found in his case histories Freud suggested that the more successful the treatment, the less scientific value there is in the record of an analysis. This is another example of the tension in Freud's work between the therapeutic endeavour and what he liked to call 'the science of unconscious mental processes' (1925d: 255). Just as psychoanalysis (in Freud's eyes) might prove in the end to be less valuable as a therapeutic tool and more useful as a way of understanding, so too a case that took a shorter time to complete, even if it was successful, yielded less in the way of knowledge about the unconscious processes that were part and parcel of it, than if it were to go on unresolved. Elsewhere Freud also commented on the difference between research and treatment:

> Analytic work certainly has a name for combining research with treatment. But beyond a certain point, the technique used by the former is in conflict with the latter ... The treatment's prospects will be harmed by a process designed to be useful to science ... By contrast the most successful cases are those in which you proceed as though you have no plan, allowing yourself to be taken by surprise at every turn, and constantly maintaining an open mind, free of presuppositions. (1912e/2002: 35–6)

Case-study: Elisabeth von R.

Freud's analysis of Elisabeth von R. is a good example of this open-mindedness, at least inasmuch as Freud was genuinely puzzled throughout much of the work, and informed as much by accident as by any theory as to the underlying cause of her difficulties. When he worked with her he had little in the way of presupposition or investment in his theories, both of which could have obscured his interpretation of the symptoms and verbal material that the patient presented. The case is an example of his refusal to accept partial answers, or to accept temporary relief of the patient's presenting symptoms as an indication of cure. There are places in the course of therapy where he might have chosen to stop, but he was convinced that they had not together arrived at the root of the patient's difficulties. As in other cases in *Studies on Hysteria* Freud provides a chronological account of the course of treatment. His later case-studies tend to start with a few sessions in similar detail, but move into theoretical constructions based on the sum of the evidence collated from later sessions as well. In the case of the Rat Man, for example, the first eleven sessions are mentioned with varying amounts of detail, but the greater part of the case history, even before it moves into the theoretical section, consists mainly of a study of the major themes contained within the material (Freud, 1909d/2002: 123–202).

In 1892 Freud was asked to examine a twenty-four-year-old woman, introduced to the reader as Elisabeth von R., who had been suffering from pains in her legs, and who had difficulty walking. In common with many other patients in Freud's practice at that particular time, her presentation was physical – partial paralysis of her limbs – one of the indications of what is known as 'hysterical conversion'. The doctor referring her to Freud told him that Elisabeth had suffered a series of family misfortunes – her father had died, her mother had undergone a serious eye operation, and a married sister had died of heart trouble during her second pregnancy. Much of the nursing of these family members had fallen to Elisabeth.

Freud's medical practice led him to start by examining her physical condition, although some years later Freud was to recommend that therapy should not be carried out by anyone who had another type of relationship with a patient, professionally or socially, including 'a different kind of therapy undertaken earlier' (1913c/ 2002: 47). In the 1913 paper he wrote that should the patient, in the course of analysis, require medical treatment 'it is much more appropriate to call in a non-analytic colleague rather than undertake this kind of care oneself' (1913c/2001: 137). In another of the papers on technique he wrote that analytic treatment requires physical abstinence (1915a/2002: 72). The early confusion of boundaries in Freud's medical and psychoanalytic roles was not one that could be sustained, although of course there are interesting blurrings of boundaries later, such as the analysis of his daughter Anna, who herself was involved in the nursing care of her father, just as were many of the young women in those early case histories.

Freud gathered that Elisabeth's pain was indefinite. The focus for the pain was in her right thigh. He noticed that when he applied pressure to the painful area, her face seemed to show more pleasure than pain, as though there was something erotic about being touched. Although he felt that there might be some organic explanation for the pain, he also observed that Elisabeth was 'dwelling on something else, of which the pains were only an accessory phenomenon – probably on thoughts and feelings, therefore, which were connected with them' (Freud and Breuer, 1895d: 204). He embarked for a while on physical treatment, which brought some slight improvement; but when, 'after four weeks of my pretence treatment, I proposed the other method and gave her some account of its procedure and mode of operation, I met with quick understanding and little resistance' (1895d: 205).

This preliminary medical approach, followed by the cathartic method, prefigures a rather different two-part approach in Freud's later practice:

> In quite a number of cases, indeed, an analysis falls into two clearly dis-
> tinguishable phases. In the first, the physician procures from the patient
> the necessary information, makes him familiar with the premises and
> postulates of psychoanalysis, and unfolds to him a construction of the
> genesis of his disorder as deduced from the material brought up in
> the analysis. In the second phase the patient himself gets hold of the
> material put before him: he works on it, recollects what he can of the
> apparently repressed memories, and tries to repeat the rest as if he were
> in some way living it over again. In this way he can confirm, supple-
> ment and correct the inferences made by the physician. (1920a: 377)

For our present purposes the course of therapy with Elisabeth might be divided into four phases – catharsis, resistance, denoue-ment and outcome.

Catharsis

The preliminary stage of physical treatment over, Freud's major work with Elisabeth was what he called 'cathartic treatment' (Freud and Breuer, 1895d: 206). This was 'the first full-length analysis of a hysteria undertaken by me' (1895d: 206), largely with-out the use of hypnosis. Freud wrote that he 'arrived at a proce-dure which I later developed into a regular method and employed deliberately. This procedure was one of clearing away the patho-genic psychical material layer by layer, and we liked to compare it with the technique of excavating a buried city' (1895d: 206). Elisabeth was asked to tell Freud what she knew, while he noted places where there was obscurity in her narrative, or broken links in a chain of events (1895d: 207). In this way Freud was able to locate possible points of resistance, whether in consciously with-holding of information or in unconsciously forgetting.

Elisabeth began talking freely about herself and about some of her memories. She was the youngest of three daughters, tenderly attached to her parents, but particularly to her father, who used to say that she took the place of a son. He used to tell her to be wary of her habit of regardlessly telling people the truth. This particular reference to her father may have been an example of what was later known as 'displacement', expressing through her father's warning some of her own reservations about 'telling the truth regardlessly' to Freud. Although he might later have recognized this possible reference to himself, he does not seem to have identified it either at the time or in writing the case history.

Her father developed a heart disease, and Elisabeth played a leading role in nursing him for eighteen months, sleeping in his room, and forcing herself to appear cheerful. She remembered getting the pains for a day and a half sometimes in the last six months of nursing him, but they had passed off. It was not in fact until two years after his death that she became incapable of walking on account of the pain in her legs (1895d: 208).

Freud continued to gather all the history that Elisabeth could provide. A year after her father's death her elder sister married a man who showed some lack of consideration to Elisabeth's mother. Her second sister also married a much more acceptable man; and their first child became Elisabeth's favourite. However, misfortune befell again, because Elisabeth had to nurse her mother after an eye operation. After her mother had recovered, all three sisters and their families went on holiday together. She told Freud that it was during this holiday that her pains really started. She was advised to take treatment at a spa, which she visited with her mother. While she was away her second sister became pregnant again, but her condition gave cause for concern. Elisabeth and her mother hurried back to see her, but arrived too late. They arrived to find the sister dead. Her brother-in-law was inconsolable, and withdrew from his wife's family.

Resistance

This much Elisabeth was able to tell Freud quite freely, although talking brought no relief to her pains. Freud felt there was something else that had not yet emerged. It is at this point that the therapy entered a second phase, with Freud making his first reference to an example of resistance, one that nearly took him in. He had at the start of the therapy agreed with the patient that he would only use hypnosis if her memories became difficult to access. He tried it at this point but it did not work. He tried his pressure technique, placing hands on her head and asking her questions. At first this brought more material, although on other occasions Elisabeth maintained that no thoughts occurred to her. At first Freud 'allowed myself to be led into breaking off the work: it was an unfavourable day; we would try another time' (1895d: 222). However, Freud noticed patterns about such times, including Elisabeth's face betraying the fact that some mental process was nevertheless going on within her, even when she had nothing to say:

I resolved, therefore, to adopt the hypothesis ... that she was not always prepared to communicate ... and tried to suppress once more what had been conjured up. Either she was applying criticism to the idea ... on the ground of its not being important enough or of its being an irrelevant reply to the question she had been asked; or she hesitated to produce it because – she found it too disagreeable to tell ... I no longer accepted her declaration that nothing had occurred to her, but assured her that something must have occurred to her. ... In the course of this difficult work I began to attach a deeper significance to the resistance offered by the patient to the reproduction of her memories and to make a careful collection of the occasions on which it was particularly marked. (1895d: 223–4)

Freud had an eye for detail. He had the ability of noting the apparently insignificant, and of recalling it at a later point in therapy. This ability was a major factor in his skill in making constructions and interpretations. Nothing was irrelevant to him. The concern for detail lay behind the rule of free association (speaking everything that came to mind, however obscure it might seem). Similarly, the details of signs of resistance were significant, because they might in turn reveal clues to the very situations they were designed to hide. That Elisabeth was resistant seemed to indicate the presence of painful feelings that could not be allowed into consciousness.

It was part of Freud's genius to recognize that in therapy every barrier is also a potential pointer, not simply a nuisance to be accepted or even to be bypassed. In working with Elisabeth von R. he identified the value of resistance; later he was to realize the similar value implicit in the phenomenon of transference. Rather than see resistance and transference simply as interfering with the progress of therapy, Freud identified them as indispensable means for understanding more of what was going on with the patient, and in the patient's relationships.

During this phase of treatment Elisabeth sometimes spoke freely, but at other times she showed signs of resistance. Freud's response to the latter seems to have been a somewhat over-authoritative demand that she reveal what she was concealing from him (1895d: 223). She then remembered going to a party at the family's insistence, when she was nursing her father. She recalled how she had met a young man there of whom she was already fond; how she had stayed too late, and hurried home to find her father worse; and how she had reproached herself for enjoying the young man's company. This is an example of a typical conflict arising from the presence of two opposing feelings – Elisabeth's wish to care for her father, and her wish to stay with the young man; and also her ambivalence about wanting to care for her father, but also feeling resentful towards him for taking a turn for the worse when she was not around. The term 'ambivalence' (typically feelings of love and hate towards the same object or person) was first suggested by Jung's superior Bleuler, but gratefully adopted by Freud (1912b/2002: 27).

Conflicts about ambivalent feelings often lie at the root of personal difficulties, although this particular conflict did not seem related to the onset of the pains. Nevertheless Elisabeth now volunteered that the pain in her right thigh was one that she understood – it was the place where her father's leg had rested when she rebandaged it each day. Furthermore, as Freud delightfully puts it:

> her painful legs began to 'join in the conversation' during our analyses. ... As a rule the patient was free from pain when we started work. If, then, by a question or by pressure upon her head I called up a memory, a sensation of pain would make its first appearance, and this was usually so sharp that the patient would give a start and put her hand to the painful spot. (1895d: 217)

The pains would not disappear until the memory had been fully expressed.

Further memories came back to Elisabeth during this period of therapy, such as standing at the door, feeling rooted to the ground (a form of paralysis perhaps?), both when her father was brought home with his heart- attack, and when she entered the room where her sister had already died. She remembered a walk in which her brother-in-law was persuaded to join Elisabeth by her sister, who felt too unwell to join them. She recalled sitting at the holiday resort after her sister and brother-in-law had left, with a burning wish that she might be as happy as her sister. Together she and Freud began to link more and more occasions to different areas of her pain, and to the different times she had experienced pain.

Denouement

'The patient was better. She had been mentally relieved and was now capable of successful effort. But her pains had manifestly not been removed; they recurred from time to time, and with all their old severity' (1895d: 224). So comments Freud at the beginning of the final period of the treatment. They still had not got to the deepest level of difficulty. Freud had an idea of what it might be about but he had no real confirmation of it. He waited.

It was in fact a chance occurrence that decided the matter for him. One day while Elisabeth was with him, a man's footsteps and voice were heard in the next room. Elisabeth got up and asked if they could finish for the day; but clearly the pain had come back because her face and gait showed it. Freud writes: 'My suspicion was strengthened by this and I determined to precipitate the decisive explanation' (1895d: 224). The man whom she and Freud had heard outside the room was her brother-in-law.

Freud used this opportunity to present his own construction, and as he did so he encountered strong protests from Elisabeth, suggesting that his confrontation of her might have been too abrasive, even if it appears to have been effective. He took her back through various memories, putting them together in a single construction: to the affection she saw in her second sister's marriage; to the pains that followed her sitting wishing to be as happy as her sister; to the news of her sister's illness reaching her at the spa; and to the increase in the violence of her pains when she looked upon her dead sister, when the thought occurred to her (as Freud surmised) 'like a flash of lightning in the dark "Now he is free again and I can be his wife"' (1895d: 226).

It seemed clear, at least to Freud. Elisabeth had almost succeeded in fending off 'an incompatible idea. ... This girl felt towards her brother-in-law a tenderness whose acceptance into consciousness was resisted by her whole moral being. She succeeded in sparing herself the painful conviction that she loved her sister's husband, by inducing physical pains in herself instead' (1895d: 227). She cried aloud when Freud said, 'So for a long time you had been in love with your brother-in-law'. She complained of dreadful pains, and protested that it was not true, that she had been talked into it, that she was incapable of such wickedness, and that she could never forgive herself if she had thought that. Freud tried to console her by reassuring her 'that we are not responsible for our feelings, and that her behaviour, the fact that she had fallen ill in these circumstances, was sufficient evidence of her moral character' (1895d: 227). It was a long time before such appeals to reason made any impression upon her.

Even if we discount some of the forcefulness in this account as being part of a dramatic narrative with which Freud also tries to persuade the reader of the significance of unconscious wishes, there is at the very least the possibility of suggestion in Elisabeth's acceptance of Freud's construction. Despite his calming reassurance of her at the end of the session, he had piled inference upon inference on her when she was clearly in a state of distress. Certainly in the later papers on technique Freud warns against the analyst imposing ideas upon the patient. 'It is not difficult for a practised analyst to identify clearly the suppressed wishes of a patient, even from the nature of his complaints and his case history (1913c/2002: 60). He especially warns against plunging in with interpretations when the patient is a 'stranger', but adds, 'even in the later stages of the treatment you must be careful not to communicate the explanation of a symptom or the interpretation of a desire until the patient has reached the point where he is only a short step away from seizing this explanation for himself'. Presumably he is not referring to his work with Elisabeth, in the passage where he acknowledges his mistakes: 'In earlier years I had plenty of opportunity to discover that communicating an explanation prematurely put a premature end to the therapy, both because of the resistances it suddenly aroused, and because of the relief the explanation brought with it' (1913c/2002: 60).

Nevertheless, the poet and novelist D.M. Thomas, who draws upon this case in his novel *The White Hotel* (1981), and is an admirer of Freud, observes that Freud uses obvious sexual imagery when he describes his treatment of Elisabeth:

> When he compels Elizabeth von R. to confront the hidden knowledge that she had been in love with her brother-in-law, his style becomes erotically charged: ... forced itself irresistibly upon her once more, like a flash of lightning in the dark ... the analyst's labours were richly rewarded ... fending off ... excitations ... resistance ... a shattering effect on the poor girl ... the most frightful pains ... one last desperate effort to reject ... we probed ... I was able to relieve her once more. ... Apart from the analytical terminology, it is the style of mildly sadistic pornography. (Thomas, 1982: 8)

Freud somewhat optimistically assumes in one of the very last papers he wrote that the patient is always able to reject the wrong construction, and that no harm will be done if the analyst makes a mistake – something he acknowledges is always a possibility. He advises that when the analyst realizes that a mistake has been made, 'at some appropriate moment we can tell the patient as much, without loss of authority' (1937d/2002: 215). Nevertheless, although a mistaken construction may have wasted time, he does not think it touches the patient. Freud believes that 'the analyst must have behaved very incorrectly' (1937d/2002: 216) before the danger arose of leading the patient astray by suggestion. He adds, 'Without vainglory, I can say that such an abuse of "suggestion" has never once occurred through my career' (1937d/2002: 216). He fails, at least in this paper, to recognize just how powerful the authority of the therapist can be when the patient is looking for an answer, especially when any answer will do.

Outcome

The fact that Elisabeth's therapy did not finish there is one indication that Freud's sense of timing was not disastrously wrong. He took hold of this central explanation, which had previously been unconsciously disowned, and was then consciously denied. He took Elisabeth back through her memories in order to set her forbidden thought in context. 'We probed into the first impressions made on her in her relations with her brother-in-law, the beginnings of the feelings for him which she had kept unconscious' (1895d: 227–8). These included the brother-in-law thinking that Elisabeth was her sister the first time he visited the house; and an occasion when her sister half-jokingly said, 'You two would have suited each other perfectly' – showing that Elisabeth's feelings may have been dormant for a long time. This process of going through memories a second time (or even more often) Freud called 'working through'. Working through partly involves going over a story and seeing it from different angles; it partly involves abreaction, by repeating the story until it ceases to exert the same emotional hold; and it partly means overcoming resistance to full acknowledgement of the situation: 'this working through of the resistances may in practice turn out to be an arduous task for the subject of the analysis and a trial of patience for the analyst' (1914g/2001: 155).

Freud often found himself advising beginning therapists that what appeared to be lack of progress in treatment was in fact a sign of heightened resistance, aroused because therapy was getting closer to repressed impulses (1914g/2001: 155). In Elisabeth's case, however, 'the analyst's labours were richly rewarded' (Freud and Breuer, 1895d: 226). Her condition, which had fluctuated throughout analysis in relation to the degree of conflict between her wishes and her resistance, once more improved. There was no more sign of the pains. Apart from one episode after she had stopped seeing Freud, and a few minor occasional pains, Freud concludes his case history of Elisabeth with the words:

> In the spring of 1894 I heard that she was going to a private ball for which I was able to get an invitation, and I did not allow the opportunity to escape me of seeing my former patient swirl past in a lively dance. Since then, by her own inclination, she has married someone unknown to me. (1895d: 230)

It might be expected that Freud would cite successful cases in order to prove the value of his therapeutic method. His own assessment of outcome can be checked in some instances through subsequent information from the patient. Gay records how

Elisabeth von R., for example, later told her daughter that she 'discounted Freud's solution of her neurotic symptoms. ... He had tried "to persuade me that I was in love with my brother-in-law, but that wasn't really so".' Nevertheless, her daughter has added that Freud's account of her mother's family history was 'substantially correct and her mother's marriage was happy' (Gay, 1989: 72). Freud claimed similar success for his treatment of the patient known as the Rat Man: 'with the emergence of this solution the rat delirium went away' (1909d/2002: 172). A footnote added in 1923 similarly records the restoration of the patient's mental health, and that 'like so many other promising and estimable young men [he was] killed in the Great War' (1909d/2002: 202).

Freud makes more modest claims in other case-studies. In *The Psychogenesis of a Case of Homosexuality in a Woman* (1920a) Freud began by outlining his misgivings about taking on the patient at all because it was her parents who wanted Freud to see her. Later, he described her intellectual resistance, which he had no way of removing. The young woman participated fully in the analysis with her mind, but her emotions were absent. At one point, when Freud explained a specially important part of his understanding of her, she replied, 'How very interesting', as though, as Freud puts it, she was a grand lady being taken round a museum and glancing through her lorgnette at objects about which she was completely indifferent (1920a: 390)!

It seemed, writes Freud, as though nothing resembling a transference to himself had been effected – making therapy incredibly difficult, because transference is a key element. But of course some kind of relationship to the analyst must exist, and this relationship is, he writes, 'almost always transference from an infantile one' (1920a: 391). 'In reality', he continues, 'she transferred to me the sweeping repudiation of men which had dominated her ever since the disappointment she had suffered from her father' (1920a: 391). This sort of bitterness is easy to gratify with a therapist, simply by rendering all the therapist's endeavours futile, and refusing to change. So as soon as Freud recognized the girl's attitude to her father, he himself broke off the therapy, and advised her parents that if they thought therapy was the right course, it should be continued by a woman therapist (1920a: 391).

Of the first case which Freud published, Emmy von N., Freud recorded that 'the therapeutic success on the whole was considerable; but it was not a lasting one' (Freud and Breuer, 1895d: 163). In a long footnote at the end of the case, added in 1924, Freud brought Emmy's history up to date, with an account of a letter to him from her daughter, in which relationships were clearly very strained. There was reference to other unsuccessful attempts at treatment by other doctors, many ending the same way as with Freud: apparent recovery, followed by a quarrel with the doctor and leaving with the symptoms having returned. 'It was a genuine instance of the "compulsion to repeat"' (1895d: 167–8).

An Eye for Detail

What emerges from Freud's longer case histories, and from many of his smaller examples, is his eye for detail. In the *Introductory Lectures* Freud justifies its importance, against those who protest,

> there are so many problems in the wide universe, as well as within the narrower confines of our minds, so many marvels in the field of mental disorders, which require and deserve to have light thrown upon them, that it does really seem gratuitous to waste labour and interest on such trivialities. (1916–17: 51)

He replies:

> If you were a detective engaged in tracing a murder, would you expect to find that the murderer left his photograph behind at the place of the crime, with his address attached? or would you not necessarily have to be satisfied with comparatively slight and obscure traces of the person you were in search of? So do not let us under-estimate small indications; by their help we may succeed in getting on the track of something bigger. (1916–17: 52)

A good illustration of Freud's eye for detail, and of the extraordinary number of associations he was able to draw out of a single phrase, is found in the case history of the Rat Man (1909d/2002). The pseudonym given to this patient owes its origin to an obsessional anxiety arising from the patient's hearing a story in the army of a torture in which rats were placed in an upturned can on a soldier's bottom, and gnawed their way out through his anus.

Freud traced the association both to this story and to the word 'rat' in various ways: the patient's father had been something of a gambler (in German a *Spielratte*); the rats in the anus may have reminded the patient of enemas he had as a boy when he had roundworms; the patient reacted to the word 'rats' (in German *Ratten*) with the word 'Raten', meaning instalments, a reference to money and to a debt he owed; the rats were also symbols of his dread of syphilitic infection; the rat was a symbol of the male sexual organ, which in turn could be seen like a worm, and the large roundworm inside him as a child; the rat is a dirty animal, feeding on excrement. Also woven into the patient's association was the verb *heiraten* ('to marry'), reflecting his anxiety about a woman he wished to marry against his father's wishes. Rats had yet another meaning for him, that of 'children' (the Pied Piper) – the woman he wanted to marry was unable to have children, yet he was extraordinarily fond of them, and this was another reason for his hesitation in marrying her. Further significance was given to the word from recalling an occasion when the patient visited the father's grave and saw what he thought was a rat gliding over the tomb. He assumed it had come out of his father's grave and had been feeding off the corpse. The notion of the rat was also connected with an animal with sharp teeth that gnaws and bites, and the patient as a child had been severely reprimanded by his father for biting when he was in a rage. Freud commented upon the original story of the rats told to the patient, that it was a complex stimulus word, which had given rise to many thoughts, which had to be repressed, in turn giving rise to his obsessional anxieties (1909d/2002: 159–72).

A further example of Freud's mastery of detail from the same case concerns a prayer which the patient used to use to ward off erotic thoughts about the woman he loved. In order to shorten the prayer (which had to be said over and over again in an obsessive ritual), the patient took the first letter of every line, and added the word 'Amen' to the end, using it as a type of magic spell – 'Glejsamen' – against every evil thought. In fact the letters spelled out, in the form of an anagram, the woman's name 'Gisela'. Since the word *Samen* in German means 'semen', the patient's phrase for warding off erotic thoughts consisted of a version of the woman's name, with 'semen' added. In trying to get rid of erotic thoughts, he in fact verbally masturbated with her (1909d/2002: 182). This way of thinking also illustrates the 'return of the repressed': that in the very formula of resistance to erotic thoughts, he in fact gave some expression to them.

Aspects of these constructions may seem far-fetched to many readers, although some will no doubt find fascination in the way Freud plays with words, not in any attempt to force intellectual conviction, but in search of some understanding which is ultimately convincing to the patient. It is up to patients, as Freud wrote in his paper *Constructions in Analysis*, whether they say 'Yes' or 'No', although no reply is clear-cut: 'A direct "Yes" from the analysand is ambiguous … The patient's "no" is equally ambiguous, and in fact even less usable than his "Yes".' What really is of greatest interest as a response is 'an expression you hear in more or less unchanging form, from the most varied people. It runs: I have never (would never have) thought (of) that' (1937d/2002: 216–17).

There are enough examples in Freud's writing of a scepticism about his own ideas to be certain that he did not swallow his theories and constructions nearly as readily as many of those who followed him.

Transference

Describing the problem of the emotional relationship between analyst and patient, Freud recorded an event that led to him abandoning hypnosis:

> It related to one of my most acquiescent patients, with whom hypnotism had enabled me to bring about the most marvellous results, and whom I was engaged in relieving of her suffering by tracing back her attacks of pain to their origins. As she woke up on one occasion, she threw her arms around my neck. The unexpected entrance of a servant relieved us from a painful discussion, but from that time onwards there was a tacit understanding between us that the hypnotic treatment should be discontinued. I was modest enough not to attribute the event to my own irresistible personal attraction. (1925d: 210–11)

Freud's modesty should not obscure that he was a handsome figure, and that for many people who met him or worked with him he was an inspiring figure. Helene Deutsch (1940: 185) describes how his pupils saw him: 'To this circle Freud was not alone the great teacher; he was the luminous star on the dark road of a new science, a dominating force that brought order into a milieu of struggle.' Transference is only a partial explanation.

The patient's emotional response to the analyst is frequently caricatured in the phrase 'falling in love with the therapist', but transference feelings consist of much more than love. Although Freud devoted a paper to the practical problem of transference love (1915a/2002), he referred in a more theoretical paper on transference (1912b/2002) to its positive and negative aspects, as well as to Bleuler's concept of 'ambivalence' – positive and negative feelings towards the analyst. These two expressions of transference need to be treated differently. Positive transference is further divided into friendly affectionate feelings, which are permitted into consciousness, and 'the type that comes from those that remain unconscious' – nearly always of erotic origin. The affectionate positive feelings do not need to be seen as resistance, and in fact they often assist therapy. The latter, and other more negative feelings are more in the nature of a resistance (1912b/2002: 25–6).

In his case-studies Freud did not refer to transference as much as one might expect given the prominence of the phenomenon in his writing on technique, and the centrality given to it in psychodynamic practice during Freud's lifetime and subsequently. Perhaps the explanation of this partly lies in the majority of the case-studies having being written prior to the later significance attached to the concept. The one case-study written after the papers on technique (of which two deal exclusively with transference) refers more explicitly to the transference relationship between the patient and himself. The young lesbian woman I referred to above is understood by Freud to transfer 'to me her sweeping repudiation of men which had dominated her ever since the disappointment she had suffered from her father' (1920a: 391). Similarly, in a dream which she brought to analysis, she expressed her longing for a man's love and for children. The patient had continuously been deceiving her father prior to entering treatment, and Freud might expect a similar transferred relationship to himself. As he describes: 'Warned through some slight impression or other ... [I] told her one day that I did not believe these dreams, that I regarded them as false or hypocritical, and that she intended to deceive me just as she habitually deceived her father. I was right; after I had made this clearer, this kind of dream ceased' (1920a: 392). It may have ceased, of course, because Freud had been so dismissive and disbelieving. But it is always easier to be wise in these matters after the event.

Freud understands neurosis as being a 'compulsion to repeat' (1914g/2001: 150). This compulsion to repeat also appears in the relationship between the therapist and patient. Transference of feelings from earlier figures in the patient's experience to the present therapeutic situation is part of the process of repetition. Repeating 'implies conjuring up a piece of real life' (1914g/2001: 152). By handling the transference responsibly the therapist is able to render the compulsion to repeat harmless, and indeed to turn it into something useful, 'by giving it the right to assert itself in a definite field'. Freud sees the original presenting symptoms as being replaced by symptoms that arise in relation to the therapist. This is what he means by the replacement of the original neurosis by a transference neurosis (1914g/2001: 154). 'The transference thus creates an intermediate region between illness and real life, through which the transition from one to the other is made. ... It is a piece of real experience' (1914g/2001: 154).

Despite the positive value attached to transference in the 1914 paper, a year earlier Freud was writing about the use of transference in a different way. It was primarily a resistance, and as such it need only be referred to if it showed itself in such a form. 'As long as the patient continues to communicate and to associate freely, the topic of transference should not be raised. You should hold back this most delicate procedure until the transference has become a resistance' (1913c/2002: 59, Freud's italics).

Freud's paper on transference love warns the therapist against responding to transference feelings, but also against ignoring them: neither is likely to further treatment. He also warns against preparing female patients for the emergence of love in the transference or encouraging 'them "only to fall in love with the doctor in order to move the analysis forward". I find it hard to think of a more absurd approach. The analyst thereby robs the phenomenon of its convincing spontaneous character' (1915a/2002: 69).

In issuing this warning against therapists responding to transference love, we need to remember that Freud was writing at a time when the vast majority of analysts were men, and as if such risks only came from working with women. He refers disparagingly to certain women with whom analysis is doomed to failure because they are 'of elemental passion, who will not put up with any surrogates, children of nature who will not accept the mental in place of the material' (1915a/2002: 74). That transference problems of such intractability can also arise with men he fails to recognize. His anxiety about responding to demands for love through acting out arose partly because Freud was aware of equivalent problems in analysts, known as counter-transference. Freud only referred to this term twice, and then only in passing. Counter-transference later came to include the positive value of monitoring feelings and thoughts aroused in the therapist by the client, enabling the therapist to appreciate more of the client's experience, but this shift in understanding took place some years after Freud's death.

The importance therefore now given in psychodynamic practice to the complex phenomenon of counter-transference, is not found in Freud's writing. The closest that Freud gets to using the therapist's own thoughts and feelings in a positive way is when he describes the parallel rule for the analyst to that of free association in the patient.

> Just as the analysand is required to relate everything he has picked up in the course of his self-observation … so the doctor should enable himself to use everything he hears … without introducing his own kind of censorship. … Expressed in a single formula: he should orientate his own unconscious as a kind of receptive organ towards the communicative unconscious of the patient. (1912e/2002: 37)

Aware of difficulties in the therapist, he commends the emphasis given by Jung and the Zurich school to the requirement that:

> everybody who sets out to analyse others should first have undergone analysis himself at the hands of an expert. … any analyst who has

spurned [this] precaution ... can easily be tempted to project his knowledge of his own characteristics derived from a vague self-perception, on to science as a generally valid theory. (1912e/2002: 38)

In one of his final papers Freud stressed that the true preparation of an analyst was the analysis of himself; and he went as far as to suggest that 'every analyst should periodically, about every five years, submit himself to analysis again' (1937c/2002: 204). This proposal was never taken up.

Freud's Relationship with his Patients

The traditional picture of the Freudian analyst is that of the 'blank screen' – the faceless analyst, upon whom projections may be made and towards whom transference love is sure to be experienced. Some support for this apparently distant position is found in Freud's papers on technique. He explained his use of the sofa as having many reasons:

> First, there is a personal motive, which others may share with me. I cannot bear to be stared at for eight hours a day or longer. Since I like to give myself over to my own unconscious thoughts while I listen, I do not want the patient trying to interpret my expression, nor do I want to influence what he is telling me. (1913c/2002: 55)

He wrote against the open involvement of the therapist in therapy:

> It is surely an enticing prospect for the young, keen psychoanalyst to deploy a good deal of his own individuality in order to carry the patient along with him. ... You might think it perfectly acceptable, indeed useful for the purpose of overcoming the patient's resistances, for the doctor to allow him a glimpse of his own psychological defects and conflicts and, by confiding in him about his own life enable him, enable him to enjoy parity. ... I do not hesitate to reject this kind of technique as defective. For the patient the doctor should remain opaque, and, like a mirror surface, should show nothing but what is shown to him. (1912e/2002: 38–9)

Freud agreed that it was permissible, to achieve some results in a shorter time, to combine analysis with 'a quantity of suggestive influence', but such a 'method does not belong to psychoanalysis proper' (1912e/2002: 39). However, he does not seem to have followed his own rules in this respect. This is illustrated in a number of cases, which suggest that he was far less opaque than he would have others be. In the account of the analysis of the patient known as the Rat Man, for example, Freud described how:

I do not dispute the seriousness of his case not the significance of the constructs he has embraced, but suggest that his age is very much in his favour, as in the intactness of his personality: in saying this I am making a positive comment about him, and he is visibly cheered by it. (1909d/2002: 143)

Reassurance and personal feedback were obviously not confined to Freud's work with Elisabeth.

Similar examples of Freud's obvious personal involvement in the therapeutic conversation were remembered by the patient known as the Wolf Man, when he was interviewed by Obholzer. He remembered how Freud explained to him the reason for his seating position, that a girl had once tried to seduce him when he sat elsewhere. Freud sometimes gave his views: 'he discussed painting and that a son of his had wanted to become a painter, that he gave up that idea and became an architect' (Obholzer, 1980: 33–4). Freud helped him out occasionally with money (Obholzer, 1980: 60–1). The Wolf Man remains 'Freud's own fascinating and rich case history' (Roazen, 1979: 170), and it seems that both the Wolf Man and Freud held each other in high regard: the Wolf Man because he admired Freud's manner and intellect, Freud because he saw the Wolf Man as 'ideally suited to exhibit his "uncomfortable" theories' (Gay, 1989: 286). The closeness of the bond between them may partly explain some of Freud's contributions, personal and financial.

It is also clear that Freud was far from an opaque mirror in the extent to which he explained his ideas and his thinking to his patients. He records a long intervention in which he explained the psychological differences between the conscious and the unconscious: 'To illustrate my brief statements ... I refer to the antiquities displayed in my consulting room' (1909d/2002: 142). The conversation goes on in some detail: 'He thought ... I reply ... I confirm ... I replied that I entirely agree' (1909d/2002: 142). It was a long discussion, relevant to the patient, but with each informing and learning from the other. I have already suggested above that transference is not the only explanation for Freud's attraction to patients and pupils; as Lampl-de-Groot describes, it was when working with Freud that she realized that in addition to the transference relationship, there was a 'real' relationship between the patient and the analyst. She writes: 'I feel that Freud's carefully selected alternation of "strict neutrality" and human relatedness has definitely influenced my personal attitude and behavior as an analyst' (1976: 284).

Explanations and Interpretations

Although Freud must have explained his theories to his patients, sometimes as part of the first phase of treatment (1920a: 377), he warns against making interpretations on the basis of theory. His essay on the uses of dreams in analysis (1911e/2002) clearly distinguishes practical technique from the scientific study of dreams made in his *Interpretation of Dreams* (1900a): 'Anyone starting out from a theoretical approach to dream interpretation and coming into analytical practice will want to maintain his interest in the contents of dreams, and as far as possible perfect his interpretation of every dream the patient recounts to him. But he will soon find out that he is working under completely different conditions now.' (1911e/2002: 13). Dream-interpretation must not take precedence over the fundamental rule that the first thing that comes into the patient's mind must be dealt with first. Dreams cannot be completely analysed, and in any case it does not matter, because any content in them not brought into consciousness in one session is sure to appear again later, as long as it remains relevant.

Freud himself obviously interpreted some dreams without the full agreement of his patient: the Wolf Man gives an example of this (Obholzer, 1980: 35). But in his essay on handling dreams he again warns against it. The skilful dream-interpreter 'will feel tempted to use his dream interpretation to the full and tell every patient everything he has deduced from his dreams. This methodological tendency represents a considerable deviation from the standard treatment' (1911e/2002: 16). Freud firmly states that 'it is one thing for the doctor to know something, and another for the patient to do so' (1911e/2002: 17–18).

He expands upon this remark in one of the other papers on technique (1913c/2002). He recalls there that in the early days of analysis he took an 'over-intellectualized' view of the situation. 'We rated the patient's knowledge very highly, hardly distinguishing it from our own' (1913c/2002: 61). Freud remarks what good fortune it was if some information on the patient's history came from an outside source; and how he immediately conveyed such information and proof of the correctness of his interpretation to the patient, hoping for a certain end to the neurosis and the conclusion of treatment. 'It was a bitter disappointment when the anticipated success did not follow' (1913c/2002: 61). Freud goes on to comment on how strange it appears that a patient can consciously know a fact, and yet not know it at all in any deeper sense. It is only the recognition of the importance of the unconscious which helps resolve this puzzle. Freud's analogy is a delightful one, typical of his superb style:

> It is just as though the Ministry of Justice has issued an order to deal with juvenile transgressions in a particular, lenient way. Until this order comes to the atttention of individual local courts, or if local magistrates have no intention of obeying the order but just go on dispensing justice as they see fit, then there can be no change in the treatment of individual juvenile delinquents. (1913c/2002: 62)

Although Freud's ability to think about the mysteries of existence meant so much to him, he saw dangers in an approach that relied too heavily upon the patient's intellectual co-operation. He counsels against giving advice, or suggesting ways of sublimating that cut off patients from 'the easiest and most accessible kinds of gratification of their drives' (1912e/2002: 40). He firmly states that 'it is wrong to give the analysand tasks to do, such as concentrating his memory, thinking about a particular period of his life, etc.'; and he also dislikes 'recommending psychoanalytical reading to aid my patients. I require that they should learn personally, at first hand' (1912e/2002: 41).

The Limits and Limitations of Analysis

Early in his case-study of the young lesbian woman (1920a), Freud sets out some attitudes in patients that make the use of psychoanalysis unsuitable. He particularly emphasizes that the patient needs to be present through her or his own choice, and not at someone else's request; and also that the patient should be open to change, and not requiring the analysis to move in a particular direction:

> The ideal situation for analysis is when someone who is otherwise his own master is suffering from an inner conflict which he is unable to resolve alone, so that he brings his trouble to the analyst and begs for his help. The physician then works hand in hand with one portion of the pathologically divided personality, against the other party in the conflict. (1920a: 374)

Because the young woman in this instance was not herself complaining of any illness, Freud considered her unsuitable; and he was proved correct. Her homosexuality, if abhorrent to her parents, was not in his eyes a neurosis, simply a different 'variety of the genital organization of sexuality' (1920a: 375). He was also doubtful whether his methods were of any real value in the treatment of psychosis, where he saw no evidence of therapeutic results. The reason for this lack of success was that psychotic patients 'are, as a rule, without the capacity for forming a positive transference, so that the principal instrument of analytic technique is inapplicable to them' (1925d: 244). Nevertheless, Freud believed that his psychoanalytic assertions were best demonstrated in psychoses, where 'so many of the things that in the neuroses have to be laboriously fetched up from the depths are found ... on the surface, visible to every eye' (1925d: 245). In time he was to be proved wrong: his methods have been used with psychotic and borderline patients. In his judgement of the therapeutic value of psychoanalysis with severely disturbed patients, Freud is overly pessimistic, even if he acknowledges in passing that 'in this sphere all our knowledge is not yet converted into therapeutic power' (1925d: 245).

Psychoanalysis has established a reputation for lengthy treatment, with hourly sessions several times a week, over a number of years. Freud himself provides us with examples of both short-term and long-term therapy. The case of Katharina (Freud and Breuer, 1895d: 190–201) arose from a single chance meeting on a mountain summit; Elisabeth von R. was seen for about a year. The Wolf Man was seen six times a week for four and a half years, but was certainly not Freud's most lengthy analysis. Freud told how he analysed the composer Mahler for four hours in a stroll round a park in Leyden and 'if I may believe reports, I achieved much with him at that time' (Clark, 1980: 194; Roazen, 1979: 164). The analyst Ferenczi, who made his own particular and somewhat unusual contributions to technique, was analysed by Freud for three weeks in October 1914, and for a further three weeks, twice daily, in June 1916. Freud records that later Ferenczi reproached him for failing to give him a complete analysis (1937c/2002: 178), although Ferenczi's complaint was based not on the length of the analysis, but on Freud's failure to identify the negative transference (Dupont, 1995: xii).

Freud describes his own pattern of work:

> I work with my patients every day except Sundays and public holidays; that is to say, usually six days a week. For minor cases or in continuing treatment that is already well advanced, three hours a week are enough. ... If there are long intervals in the work, there is a danger of not keeping up with the actual experience of the patient, so that the treatment loses contact with the present. (1913c/2002: 49)

As to the question of duration, Freud reckoned that it is 'almost unanswerable. ... To put it bluntly, psychoanalysis always involves long stretches of time, six-month periods or whole years; longer than most sufferers expect. You therefore have a duty to inform the patient about this state of affairs before he finally opts for treatment' (1913c/2002: 49, 50). It is up to patients when they want to break off therapy. Freud comments that in the early years of his practice he used to have great difficulty persuading his patients to continue their analysis. 'Nowadays I anxiously try to persuade them to stop' (1913c/2002: 51). Increasingly, the psychoanalytic movement was to validate lengthy treatment, and so promote an elitism, whereby only relatively few patients could receive help, and then usually at great expense. It took many years before there was a return to a shortening of frequency and duration, such as is characterized by Freud's earlier practice. Certainly in Freud's later writing the inevitability of analysis as a 'lengthy task' is assumed (1937c/2002: 173), although he also acknowledged that 'in earlier years I had a large number of patients who were understandably keen on quick completion of their treatment' (1937c/2002: 180). One reason for his later longer analyses may be that Freud concentrated then on training analyses, although Momigliano comments that some of the later training analyses were short, and that 'sometimes they ended abruptly: Freud unexpectedly dismissed Helene Deutsch a year after her analysis began, telling her "perfectly frankly" that he needed her hour for an old patient who had returned (it was the Wolf Man), and adding "You do not need it, you are not neurotic"' (1987: 384). Helene Deutsch says that she tried 'to react to the situation maturely and objectively' but perhaps because she felt rejected, she suffered the first depression in her life (1973).

Freud was primarily interested in accuracy and not in therapeutic success. This comes out time and again in remarks he makes about the limitation of psychoanalysis as a method of healing:

> I have told you that psychoanalysis began as a method of treatment; but I did not want to commend it to your interest as a method of treatment but on account of the truths it contains, on account of the information it gives about what concerns human beings most of all – their own nature – and on account of the connections it discloses between the most different of their activities. As a method of treatment it is one among many, though to be sure primus inter pares. (1933a: 192)

I return to Freud's questioning of psychoanalysis as a therapeutic tool in the next chapter. It is appropriate to give some attention to Freud's more pessimistic outlook, as his late paper *Analysis Terminable and Interminable* (1937c/2002) reflects on these questions. As the editors of the Standard Edition note, 'the paper as a whole gives an impression of pessimism in regard to the therapeutic efficacy of psychoanalysis. Its limitations are constantly stressed, the difficulties of the procedure and the obstacles standing in the way are insisted upon' (1937c/2001: 211). Freud also doubted the prospects of preventing the occurrence of a fresh and different neurosis and even the return of the same neurosis that has been treated. He clearly states that to use recent analyses as evidence of successful outcome was undesirable because 'we have no means of predicting how a cure will work out in later years' (1937c/2002: 180).

Termination

The Wolf Man, whose return led Freud to push Helene Deutsch out, posed problems for Freud, leading him to write about it in *Analysis Terminable and Interminable* (1937c/2002). We have information on Freud's attempted termination of this analysis, where he mentions the use of a similar technique in other cases (1937c/2002: 175). The analysis would have lasted more than its four and half years had Freud not decided upon what was for him an unorthodox strategy. It appears that the therapy had become stuck, with the Wolf Man gently sabotaging Freud's efforts to assist change. Freud set a date for ending one year ahead, and stuck to it, believing that the Wolf Man's positive transference towards him was strong enough to ensure success. In that year the Wolf Man came to see that Freud would not give in, and 'he managed to reproduce all the memories and locate all the connections that the understanding of his early neurosis and overcoming of his present one seemed to require' (1937c/2002: 174). Freud saw his technique in this instance as a piece of blackmail, and he advised that the technique could only succeed if it was used at precisely the right point, especially since it was not desirable to extend the time limit once it had been fixed (1937c/2002: 175). Although Freud felt at the time that all had been resolved, he added a footnote to the case-study in 1923 to report that he was mistaken. The Wolf Man returned to Freud for a few months after the Great War, and was later referred by Freud to one of his women pupils.

Freud concludes that analysis never really comes to an end. There are incomplete analyses, which finish because of some external difficulties preventing the meeting of analyst and patient; but all analyses that end satisfactorily are in some sense unfinished. Freud does not deny successes, but he believes that, in general, difficulties brought on by traumatic events are more likely to be relieved than those due to constitutional factors.

In a famous phrase Freud calls analysis 'the third of those "impossible" professions in which, even before you begin, you can be sure you will fall short of complete success. The two others, known about for much longer, are education and government'

(1937c/2002: 203). He does not demand that the analyst should be perfect, although he stresses the need for personal analysis as part of the preparation for this work. Nor does Freud aim to create a type of monochromatic cloning of all patients who approach analysts for help:

> Nobody is going to set themselves the aim of ironing out all human idiosyncrasies in favour of a schematic normality, much less demand that someone who has been 'thoroughly analysed' should feel no passions and be subject to no inner conflicts. The analysis should create the optimum psychological conditions for the functioning of the I; its task will then be completed. (1937c/2002: 204)

In conclusion, it appears that Freud, writing about the termination of therapy at the end of his own life, remains alert to its difficulties, and to the doubts about its efficacy. This chapter has shown a number of examples, of which there are many more, where he is self-critical and anticipates, without always challenging, the criticisms that were made then as now of the techniques (and ideas) that he did so much to develop. He even recognizes the 'heads I win, tails you lose' argument which has beset some psychoanalytic repudiation of objections to its theoretical stance – indeed, he uses those very words in English in the German text (1937d/2002: 211). He accepts the possibility that 'the analysis achieves for neurotics what the healthy person does for himself without this help' (1937c/2002: 182).

It is difficult to know whether Freud's final assessment sprung from his characteristic pessimism or from his intellectual realism. What is more certain is that when it comes to the type of criticisms made of his theories and techniques, to which I turn in the next chapter, Freud has often been there before. He did not always refute critics, especially on the question of results. And without any shadow of doubt, looking ahead to the final chapter, it is clear that despite some overstatement that is at times counteracted by Freud's own approach to the work, much of what he developed by way of technique has continued to make a positive contribution to the practice of therapy and counselling, just as his theories have exerted a profound influence on twentieth-century Western culture.

4

Criticisms and Rebuttals

If some traces of the autocratic pose,
the paternal strictness be distrusted, still
clung to his utterance and features,
it was a protective coloration

for one who'd lived among enemies so long:

W.H. Auden: 'In Memory of Sigmund Freud'

Psychoanalytic Criticism and Criticism of Freud

There can be little doubt, whatever one makes of Freud, that his theories pervade the intellectual climate of western culture. This will become clear in Chapter 5. It has indeed been suggested that we live in a world 'in which the ideas of Freud have become a part of the spiritual air we breathe' (Graf, 1942: 476). Yet even taking a phrase such as this, we have to ask who wrote it, and what was his intellectual relationship, as well as his emotional relationship to Freud. Graf was in fact a young man when he met Freud, and his article, written many years later, is full of admiration, at times close to idealization of Freud. But Graf is not without criticism – he relates this, for example:

> He permitted no deviations from his orthodox teaching. Subjectively, Freud was of course right, for that which he worked out with so much energy and sequence, and which was as yet to be defended against the opposition of the world, could not be rendered inept by hesitations, weakening, and tasteless ornamentations. Good-hearted and considerate though he was in private life, Freud was hard and relentless in the presentation of his ideas. When the question of his science came up, he would break with his most intimate and reliable friends. If we do consider him as a founder of a religion, we may think of him as a Moses full of wrath and unmoved by prayers. (1942: 471–2)

The critic therefore has to consider whether Graf was swayed by intellectual conviction, or indeed by emotional admiration, to write of Freud's ideas as 'part of the spiritual air we breathe'. Yet as soon as we ask such a question, we are already framing it in Freudian terms, looking for a psychological interpretation of the motivation behind writing such a phrase. We are tacitly admitting the validity of Freud's ideas – or at least some of them – that in this case wish fulfilment (as might be the need for a powerful and authoritative father figure for the young Graf) could be playing a part in what is in the end a statement that has the character of hyperbole more than fact. Those who value Freud's work tend to exaggerate, perhaps, its universal appeal.

Freud employed the explanation of 'unconscious resistance' in places to refute criticism of his work. He may, of course, have been right at times, when he claimed that it was useless to try and argue against critics, because the type of assertions he was making 'cannot count upon meeting with the same kind of treatment as other communications' (1914d: 79). As with aesthetic or religious phenomena, there is a sense in which the critic needs to have shared a similar experience before making assertions about analytic statements. However, some of Freud's most important critics have also been trained in psychoanalysis, yet even they have sometimes been subjected to the psychoanalytic counter-argument (not always by Freud himself) that they have not been analysed enough.

Similar problems arise in relation to the psychoanalytic concept of rationalization – although it was Ernest Jones who gave the idea greater prominence than Freud. It is a concept that is regarded, 'both by the supporters as well as by the opponents of psycho-analysis, as a paradigm of the analytical method' (Hollitscher, 1939: 230). Hollitscher describes the dilemma of rationalization in this way:

> 'How,' it is asked, 'can we prove the truth of the opinion of an analyst who claims to expose the arguments of another person as a rationalization? Who can assure us that this exposure is not, in its turn, a rationalization on the part of the analyst – and therefore also of doubtful truth – intended to oppose the arguments of the other by means of an arbitrary interpretation?' (1939: 230)

Is criticism a reasonable questioning of data and interpretation, or is it a cover for unconscious anxiety? Is the hostility to the ideas themselves or to what the ideas might stand for, threatening as they sometimes do established personal values? Thus, to take a parallel example, Darwin's theory of evolution evoked hostility and counter-argument not principally because his theory was significantly flawed, but because the theory undermined a whole fabric of theological and psychological securities, as much as it questioned existing natural science. Hollitscher observes that the answer to this dilemma is clarified when it is realized that rationalization is an observation of a process, or of a motive, but that it is not a comment suggesting incorrectness in what the patient (or the critic) has said. Thus the familiar 'heads I win, tails you lose' argument in psychoanalysis, mentioned at the close of Chapter 3, is a fallacy. I might say to a critic 'The reason why you cannot accept this idea of Freud's is because it presents an unconscious emotional difficulty for you', but such a comment, according to Hollitscher's argument, is only an observation about what motivates the critic; it is not a defence of Freud's idea. It is a pretty argument, although it suggests a distinction between different forms of discourse in the person responding to the critic that is more pure than we can imagine. Too often 'rationalization' like Freud's term 'illusion' ends up meaning 'erroneous thinking' rather than 'wish fulfilment'. Analysts have a vested interest in defending Freud's ideas. Here again we find ourselves returning to the interpenetration of thinking and emotion that is part of psychoanalytic theory.

In other words, it is hard to escape the influence of Freudian thinking, and it is tempting for the person who wishes to defend Freud and psychoanalysis to use such paradigms to confute the arguments of those who seriously question many of the basic tenets of psychoanalytic theory. And although in this chapter I set out consciously to give the critics a fair hearing, who knows how much I unconsciously 'forget' the most potent criticisms or present their arguments in ways which can more readily be refuted?

Criticism of Freud's Character

Graf's observations of Freud above are an example of the type of insight into Freud that can be used to question the reliability of Freud's theories. There has been criticism, for example, that so much of his thinking is based upon his self-analysis, tempered only by his correspondence with Fliess (Masson, 1985) and that this is an unscientific basis for a set of hypotheses (Efron, 1977). There are also arguments linking his history to his ideas, suggesting that his thinking has been distorted by his personal experiences, or by his repression of problematic areas. For example, Barron et al. (1991) trace the link between Freud's interest in the secrets of human nature, and his relationship with his mother, while other authors link his criticism of religion to his background. Thus, Freud's critique of religion, and particularly of Catholicism, is sometimes 'explained' as being due to the influence of the nurse-maid who was dismissed and sent to prison for petty theft when

Freud was two. She was a devout Roman Catholic, and she may have been 'his teacher in sexual matters' (Gay, 1989: 7; see also Rainey, 1975). Or his relationship to his mother has been held up as one of the reasons for the shortcomings in Freud's theories about women's psychology and sexuality (Orgel, 1996). Here again, far from disowning Freud's theories, such articles employ certain aspects of psychoanalytic theory to critique particular areas of Freud's thinking, although, of course, we would expect this approach from those who write from a psychoanalytic perspective. If many of Freud's ideas are creations of his own personality this need not either validate or invalidate them: once more we are looking at the close relationship between unconscious motivation and the development of thought (see also my study of thinking and belief – Jacobs, 2000).

Graf's description of Freud's response to criticism appears to support the charge often made of him that he was unable to concede he was wrong. The explanation sometimes given for this is his natural defensiveness because of the strength of the hostility shown towards him in the early years. When Freud calls religion an illusion, some critics reply that he does not see that his own thinking is open to the same charge. In fact, as a master of the Socratic dialogue, he does. Freud frequently anticipates such charges in his writing: 'I know how difficult it is to avoid illusions; perhaps the hopes I have confessed to are of an illusory nature, too' (1927c: 237). While there must have been times when he would not budge, he was also ready to admit error. In *The Future of an Illusion* he wrote: 'If experience should show – not to me, but to others after me, who think the same way – that we have been mistaken, then we will renounce our expectations' (1927c: 237). He could not legislate for his followers, and indeed some of his followers have found it much more difficult to admit Freud's mistakes; but his own intentions are clear. Similarly, the editorial footnotes in the Standard Edition and the Penguin Freud Library often draw attention to corrections Freud made to his texts when new editions were printed. He freely admits when he has made mistakes: for example, 'This is a construction which I should like explicitly to withdraw' (1925d: 248n). He was self-critical in his writing, in addition to using a style that often adopts the Socratic dialogue of proposition, criticism and response to the criticism. He was more modest about his lack of knowledge and more realistic about the worth of his ideas than is sometimes assumed. For example, in his last published work he began by stating that psychoanalysis 'makes a basic assumption', and in the next paragraph setting out 'two hypotheses' (1940a: 375–6). Even if at times much of the work reads as if it were fact, these two phrases indicate his awareness of the tentative nature of his theoretical base. Yet against this we have to balance the type of credal formula he sets out when he lists the four corner-stones of psychoanalytic theory (see p. 34) and concludes 'No one who cannot accept them all should count himself as a psychoanalyst' (1923a: 145).

Graf's description supports the contention that Freud could not allow questioning of his authority. One frequently quoted illustration occurs in Jung's autobiography where he recounts Freud's refusal to discuss details of a dream, saying to Jung 'I cannot risk my authority' (Jung, 1967: 182–3). The reason given for some of the early secessions from the psychoanalytic movement is Freud's rigidity and dogmatic leadership. While military metaphors appear in Freud's writing, and perhaps lend some support to the image of him as a general leading an army into battle, we have to be careful about making sweeping assumptions about him. Opposition by Freud towards his followers appears to have been highly selective. There are plenty of examples of his tolerance of colleagues whose theories, or even techniques, departed significantly from his own. Ferenczi's relationships with some of his patients involved much more self-disclosure and physical expression of feeling than Freud found acceptable, but this did not prevent healthy disagreement between friends, and it was only at the end of his life that Ferenczi was snubbed. Otto Rank's emphasis on birth trauma was disputed by Freud without any need to threaten Rank with expulsion from analytic circles. It was Rank who gradually drew away from Freud. Freud also disagreed strongly with Ernest Jones over questions of female sexuality, and regretted the latter's support for Melanie Klein rather than Anna Freud. But Jones remained part of the 'inner circle', and was, of course, Freud's first distinguished biographer. Freud himself was aware of the criticism of his dogmatism and replied to it in his autobiography:

> I think I can say in my defence that an intolerant man, dominated by an arrogant belief in his own infallibility, would never have been able to maintain his hold upon so large a number of intelligent people, especially if he had at his command as few practical attractions as I had. (1925d: 237)

Freud's modesty here is somewhat false, although not deliberately so: many attest to the powerfulness of his personality: Graf, for example, writes: 'Freud's pupils – all inspired and convinced – were his apostles. Despite the fact that the contrast among the personalities of this circle of pupils was great, at that early period of freudian investigation all of them were united in their respect for and inspiration with Freud' (1942: 471).

It is then fair to assert that Freud's character contained a dogmatic streak. Certainly he could be censorious, although such descriptions of his character need to be tempered by a closer examination of the text. One of the difficulties with the criticisms of Freud is that all too often they are based on secondary sources. There are frequent examples in his writing which show his openness to criticism. With reference to objections raised against part of Freud's argument in favour of the ubiquity of masturbation in infancy, he wrote: 'I admit that this argument must be abandoned. If one more edition of my *Three Essays on the Theory of Sexuality* is called for, it will not contain the sentence under attack. I will renounce my attempt at guessing the purposes of Nature and will content myself with describing the facts' (1912f/2001: 247).

Freud was aware of the dangers of speculation. The danger of untested hypotheses is in evidence when he was writing about sex distinctions in later life (1925j). This particular essay begins by stating the urgency with which he was writing about some of his findings. He could not postpone them until the necessary proof was available. He reminds the reader that he has in the past held back from publishing for four or five years. It must have seemed to him that he had only a few months to live, because he was already suffering from cancer, and would not have known how many years he was still to live. So he writes: 'time before me is limited ... if I think I see something new ... I am uncertain whether I can wait for it to be confirmed.' After referring to fellow workers who could take up his unfinished and doubtful hypotheses, and test them as once he himself did, he ends his introductory paragraphs with the sentence: 'I feel justified in publishing something which stands in urgent need of confirmation before its value or lack of value can be decided' (1925j: 331–2). It is quite possible that a creative mind such as his led him on other occasions too, rather less consciously, to pen ideas, waiting to see whether they would prove useful or not.

Other critics have pointed to Freud's bias as being a product of his age; that he was, for example, a representative of the patriarchal system which inherently places women on an inferior level. Such a criticism is axiomatic. He was writing some of his papers over one hundred years ago: the intellectual world, particularly with regard to attitudes about society, as well as in its scientific paradigms, standards of psychological proof and philosophical theories is a very different one now from his heyday. What is perhaps more remarkable is that Freud is still being criticized as much as he is – Marx, for instance, who in the middle years of the twentieth century attracted similar interest – seldom figures in the intellectual currency of the new millennium. The hold which Freud's ideas have, even where they are only simplistically understood, remains very strong.

In this respect too there is evidence that Freud was aware of certain objections that could be raised against his ideas as being limited by their social and cultural context. Here he acknowledges the possibility of explaining away opposing arguments psychologically. He seems aware of these dangers both in himself and in his method:

> It is to be anticipated that men analysts with feminist views, as well as our women analysts, will disagree with what I have said here. They will hardly fail to object that such notions spring from the 'masculinity complex' of the male and are designed to justify on theoretical grounds his innate inclination to disparage and suppress women. But this sort of psychoanalytic argumentation reminds us here, as it so often does, of Dostoevsky's famous 'knife that cuts both ways'. (1931b: 377)

At the same time we have to note that while Freud saw the possibility, later in this particular paragraph he does not appear to believe that it was influencing his present thinking.

A further psychological gloss on Freud's theories links them with his own pessimism, as well in relation to the death drive to the cultural shock of the Great War and the effect on him of the diagnosis of his cancer. Such societal and personal experiences certainly suggest the possibility of a psychological causation, although we need to be cautious here again about this type of rationalization: the huge loss of life in the Great War, in the Spanish 'flu epidemic after it, as well as the personal losses that Freud sustained in his own family and in his health may have provided the incentive to develop a concept that has value; other thinkers in many other disciplines have also come to startling insights or made important discoveries consequent upon personal experience. In any case, this particular theory was the one which many of his followers have been unable to accept – indicating that, at least in this respect, Freud does not command blind obedience in psychoanalytic circles. Kernberg has suggested that 'the idealization of Freud in psychoanalytic education is illustrated in the detailed, frequently obsessive and relatively noncritical study of his work, the invocation to Freud's ideas when new developments in the field appear to threaten one of his formulations' (1986: 810). While this may be true of many of the psychoanalytic trainings, even a cursory glance through the main journals indicates that there is lively debate about Freud's ideas, while at the same time, as Kernberg observes, as much reference to his writing as one would expect in a theologian's underpinning of argument by the Bible.

Critics from Within: the First Secessions

Questioning of Freud's ideas was present from the beginning, and perhaps it was his dogmatic refusal to shift from what appears now (and indeed in the light of his later work) an exaggerated emphasis on the centrality of sexuality that led to the secessions of Adler and Jung in the early years of the psychoanalytic movement, as well as later to those of neo-Freudians such as Fromm and Horney in the 1930s and 1940s. Such significant thinkers and practitioners cannot be regarded as psychologically unbalanced, as might be argued in the case of some followers such as Tausk and Silberer, whose suicides are sometimes claimed to be the result of Freud's rejection of them and of their ideas. So-called clashes of personality there must have been, and the critics can rightly question how it was that those who looked deep into the minds of others, and who (a few years later) urged analysis for all who practised it, could not see something of the reason for those early disputes. Jung certainly asked such a question about Freud (Jung, 1967: 191). But such questions necessarily have to be asked of Jung as well, as indeed of all parties where dispute has led to disunion. It is not psychoanalysis alone that has strong personalities, and the psychotherapy world generally has not handled disagreement as constructively as might be expected of it. As in other disciplines strong convictions can divide, and personal integrity (on both sides) sometimes makes division necessary.

Some of the most significant figures who broke with psychoanalysis, and whose work has led to the formation of separate and identifiable schools are examined in other volumes in this series. Jung, for example, questioned Freud's single-minded emphasis on sexuality: while corroborating Freud's theory of repression, Jung did not consider its cause inevitably to be sexual trauma. 'From my practice ... I was familiar with numerous cases of neurosis in which the question of sexuality played a subordinate part, other factors standing in the foreground – for example, the problem of social adaption, of oppression by tragic circumstances of life, prestige considerations and so on' (Jung, 1967: 170). Freud 'clung to a literal interpretation' (Jung, 1967: 191) of incest, although Jung's belief that it is 'a personal complication only in the rarest cases' (1967: 191) has since proved unrealistic. Nevertheless, Jung was right to look beyond sexuality to its inherent symbolism. The penis, for example, is as much a symbol of male potential for dominance and power over women as it is a sexual organ: both meanings can lead to neurotic problems.

Jung took symbols far beyond this point, constructing a theory of archetypes, which many would say is as unprovable as much of Freud's metapsychology. More immediately relevant are Jung's ideas on personality types (Casement, 2001). Freud acknowledged the value of some of Jung's work (such as word association), and Jung wrote appreciatively of Freud's 'courage to let the case material speak for itself, and in this way to penetrate into the real psychology of his patients' (Jung, 1967: 192). However, Freud was scornful of Jung's emphasis upon libido as 'spiritual', and remained adamant that the real reason for Jung's and Adler's secession was their difficulty in identifying themselves with the controversy generated by the centrality of sexuality. Freud objected to the way in which the Oedipus complex and sexuality were interpreted by Jung as 'abstract, impersonal and non-historical' (Freud, 1925d: 236) in character, and were not seen as necessary parts of the analysis of a patient's childhood.

Freud had no wish, so he said, to offer the enemies of psychoanalysis the pleasure of seeing analysts 'tearing one another limb from limb' (1914d: 109). This did not prevent him from devoting a whole chapter of the relatively short *History of the Psychoanalytic Movement* to a reply to Jung and to Adler, the other major secessionist during the early period of the psychoanalytic movement. Adler was also critical of the emphasis on sexuality, although what would now be known as 'gender issues' were to the forefront of his own theory of neurosis, that of the wish for power and for masculine domination over the feminine. Adler's 'excommunication' (Roazen, 1979: 167) from the Vienna Psychoanalytical Society certainly shows Freud in a poor light; and a bitter streak stabs its way through Freud's own history of the relationship between his own ideas and those of 'little Adler' (1914d: 111).

Freud must bear some responsibility for the acrimony that in retrospect, as much as at the time, appears to do such a disservice to scientific enquiry and debate. It is a significant feature of the ongoing psychoanalytic movement that too many important developments have led to or have had to take place through secession or splits. Again, some of those whose training began in psychoanalysis, and who in some cases remained for a long time in psychoanalytic societies, are featured in this series – for example, Carl Rogers (Thorne, 2003), Fritz Perls (Clarkson and Mackewn,

1993), Albert Ellis (Yankura and Dryden, 1994) and Eric Berne (Stewart, 1992). But Freud personally was not the direct cause of their leaving, even if his theories have been found inadequate by most of them. That such critics have in some instances been forced into founding their own schools is a mark of the difficulties that stem from the institutionalization of psychoanalysis, and the conservatism and protectionism of many of the national organizations. Institutions of all kinds frequently prevent debate and criticism, or circumscribe it, in their desire to protect their own standards and maintain the rules they have themselves set. Psychoanalysis does not always seem to have been able to contain radical disagreement. It has sometimes taken years before similar ideas to those which caused dissension have resurfaced within psychoanalysis, only then providing opportunities for the extension and revision of Freudian theory and practice. Shorter-term and aim-limited therapy is a particularly good example, treated with suspicion in the 1940s, but made respectable by the 1960s (Malan, 1963).

Freud and his Followers

Although those referred to in the section above, and the section below, may be regarded as making significant contributions to the development of psychotherapeutic ideas and practice, we may still be critical of some of those who remained clearly within the psychoanalytic camp, and yet did little more than bolster Freud's ideas against the criticism of those who wished to move them on. Freud may not directly be criticized for this, except inasmuch as in organizational terms he appears to have been less tolerant of dissension than he was when working on his own ideas. These followers made the Cause into a set of dogmas that needed to be defended. Fromm observes how tentative and cautious Freud was when presenting his new ideas for the first time. 'He made no claim for their validity, and sometimes spoke deprecatingly of their value. But the more time passed, the more hypothetical constructs turned into theories upon which new constructions and theories were built' (1980: 132). Fromm asks what happened to the original doubts. One possible answer is that 'those who built the movement were mostly pedestrian men, from the standpoint of their theoretical capacity. ... They needed a dogma in which they believed and around which they could organize the movement.' The better students, who dared to criticize, left or were squeezed out. 'Freud the teacher became the prisoner of his faithful, but uncreative disciples' (1980: 132).

D.M. Thomas, reviewing Bettelheim's *Freud and Man's Soul*, praised it as a book 'which could *rescue Freud from the Freudians* by restoring the psyche (i.e. the soul) to analysis' (Bettelheim, 1983: dustcover, my italics). We might also point to the neo-Freudians, who felt compelled to break from the more conservative psycho-analytic groups to which those who emigrated to the United States became attached: analysts such as Eric Fromm, Karen Horney, Clara Thompson, and, somewhat in a category of his own, Harry Stack Sullivan. Erik Erikson's position in relation to psychoanaly-sis is not clear: formally he remained a Freudian, although in his thinking he was more like the neo-Freudians (Erikson, 1950; see also Friedman, 1999 and Welchman, 2000). The neo-Freudians are a distinct group, who demonstrate as individuals different criti-cisms of certain aspects of Freud's theories. Fromm, for example, is more discriminating in his analysis of religion than Freud, distin-guishing authoritarian religion as having the same obsessional neurotic undermining quality that Freud had suggested, and humanitarian religion, which Fromm sees as much more positive in its potentialities. Karen Horney (Rubins, 1978) and Clara Thompson find Freud's views of women profoundly unsatisfac-tory and represent an important early feminist critique of the place of women in Freudian theory. What the neo-Freudians have in common – and in this they drew upon some of the ideas which Adler had raised about persons interacting with others in society – is radical criticism of Freud's theory of instincts or drives. They recognize, partly through their own move from Germany to the United States, that cultural and sociological factors make as impor-tant a contribution to neurosis as the family does. Guntrip describes how in the neo-Freudians 'the original Freudian biologi-cal emphasis provoked an antithetical sociological and cultural emphasis' (1961: 351).

Bocock observes that although the practice of psychoanalysis as a therapeutic technique has come a long way since Freud, it has not always altered for the better. It may get its inspiration from Freud, but 'Freud's own work is much more critical than later therapeutic techniques have become'; and sociologists can 'throw considerable light on the kinds of social, economic and cultural influences which have led therapists, analysts, counsel-lors and social workers to try and change Freud's theory and practice in the direction of social conformity' (Bocock, 1983: 134). Weinstein similarly comments that because people need the versions of reality which intellectuals provide, Marx and Freud were confirmed in their high self-regard, but they were also cut off from awareness that their intellectual constructions, like constructions in psychoanalytic therapy, did not need to be objectively true. ... And it happened, too, that many of these people, coming to [their] work from the standpoint of subjective needs and expectations, often focused attention on the wrong issues. (Weinstein, 1980: 4)

Critics from Within: the Post-Freudians

It would be misleading to give the impression that Freud's ideas could only be questioned by those who set themselves apart from the psychoanalytic institutes that were formed in different parts of the world. Psychoanalysis has proved to be a rich and fertile ground for ideas, perhaps on a scale more diverse than any other therapeutic approach. A number of important figures have changed and developed psychoanalytic theory, feeling no inner compulsion to make their position independent nor succumbing to the need to form a completely separate school of practice. Some of the leading figures in Britain have nonetheless been identified as in one sense contributing to an independent school of psychoanalytic theory (Kohon, 1986; Rayner, 1991). Major alternative theoretical positions have been developed by Melanie Klein (1932; Segal, H., 1964; Segal, J., 1992), W.R.D. Fairbairn (1952), Harry Guntrip (1961, 1968), D.W. Winnicott (1958) and Charles Rycroft (1972, 1985), all of whom are no longer living. There are others currently in Britain and elsewhere who have made similar contributions to psychoanalytic theory: for example analysts in the United States of America, such as Hartmann (1939), Jacobson (1964), Kernberg (1976) and Kohut (1971). An extremely useful clarification of many of these analysts' theoretical positions is to be found in Greenberg and Mitchell (1983). Since all these writers have remained within the mainstream psychoanalytic tradition, I reserve some of their particular contributions for the last chapter as part of Freud's ongoing influence, although here I draw upon them and others for some of the main criticisms of Freud's theory and practice.

British object relations theory, Guntrip suggests, has ('quite unintentionally') synthesized two opposing points of view, Freud's biological emphasis and the neo-Freudian sociological emphasis (1961: 351). Guntrip's main criticism of Freud centres on the latter's scientific and deterministic approach, although he recognizes that Freud's concepts were inevitably time bound. Unlike those who criticize Freud for not being *truly* scientific, Guntrip believes that psychodynamics is not a natural science, but 'calls for a new type of theory which can take account of the individuality' of the person (1961: 118). The concept of person and personality had not assumed the importance in philosophy in Freud's time that it has in later years. 'Culturally, today is the era of human personal relationships, rather than of instincts; the problem is, given innate endowment, how that is shaped by what goes on between people' (Guntrip, 1961: 50). Where Guntrip is especially critical of Freud is in his inability to stay with the speculative without turning it into the apparently factual. For example, Freud (1920g: 295) started by calling the death instinct 'speculation, often far-fetched speculation', but then apparently became convinced by his speculation and treated it as if it were fact.

Despite major changes in the way in which relationships and the structure of personality have been understood since Freud's death, there has been little obvious change within psychoanalysis itself in the techniques or practice of therapy as developed by Freud. One significant development has been the reinstatement of brief psychotherapy (Malan, 1963; Malan and Osimo, 1992; Molnos 1995; Coren, 2001). Some of Freud's early work was indeed brief (Freud and Breuer, 1895d: 190–210, is an extreme example), but when Franz Alexander (Alexander and French, 1946), on the radical left of psychoanalysis, promoted shorter-term psychotherapy following his move from Berlin to the United States in the 1930s, there was considerable criticism of the watering down of the 'pure gold' of psychoanalysis. It is important also to bear in mind that the adaptation of Freudian practice to social work and counselling settings, and to psychotherapy as distinct from psychoanalysis, has meant the widespread practice of once-weekly sessions, considerably altering the degree of dependency of the patient or client on the therapist.

In recent years there has been increasing attention to practice by analysts themselves, with criticism of traditional psychoanalytic technique. This is often more closely argued from within psychoanalytic and psychodynamic psychotherapy than the criticism is of Freudian techniques by those who do not use these approaches, who tend to rely upon a stereotypical view of psychoanalysis to support their views. In the United States, Roy Schafer has led the way in examining the nature of communication in the analytic setting (1976, 1983). In Britain, Rycroft has extended understanding of the status of the traditional Freudian interpretation, by observing that it conveys elements of the real relationship between therapist and client that are also therapeutic: 'every correct interpretation, even when it is, as it should be, entirely free of reassurance or suggestion ... also indicates that the analyst is still present and awake, that he has been listening and has understood what the patient has been talking about, that he remembers what the patient has said during the present and previous sessions – and that he has been sufficiently interested to listen and remember and understand ... surely an essential part of the healing process' (1985: 63). If this sounds like a return to basic skills of counselling (listening, remembering, understanding) such statements have to be seen as a corrective within the analytic tradition to the view 'that the analyst is an external, objective observer of the patient's intrapsychic processes, that interpretations are interventions from outside the system, and that even transference interpretations which mention the analyst are not really about him at all but about some parental image that preexisted in the patient's mind' (Rycroft, 1985: 61). Winnicott too demonstrates a quite different therapeutic approach in some recorded instances from that which might be expected of a psychoanalyst (see Jacobs, 1995: chap. 3).

Taking Rycroft's critical stance even further, and like Rycroft (who was his own analyst) eventually distancing himself from the official psychoanalytic society in Britain, Peter Lomas clearly acknowledges his debt to Freud. He lists amongst Freud's contributions to the therapeutic endeavour the importance of looking for latent meanings, the degree to which people resist latent meanings, the long time needed to uncover these meanings, a theory of decoding meaning, and a school of thought to pass findings on from one generation to another (1987: 58). In a sequence of books Lomas has recorded his increasing dissatisfaction with the orthodox analytic technique, such as the distancing of the therapist, and what seems to him like an inability to relate other than through transference interpretation. Thus, while fully able to use psychoanalytic ideas as pointers towards some understanding of what clients express, Lomas is also aware that Freudian theory can become a mythology, into which the client's communications are fitted. He is therefore extremely cautious of the oversimplification of theory; and yet as theory becomes more complex, introducing more and more variables, it also becomes less efficient as a practical tool. He goes along with the reaction in modern scientific and philosophical thinking against excessive rationality: 'Thinkers of this persuasion believe that we are unable to stand outside the world and appreciate it objectively, because we are ourselves an ingredient in it. There is no immutable reality that we can know about, all knowledge is personal and partial, gained from our unique position' (1987: 38–9). Freud's attempts to claim a scientific position come under criticism, an argument that I expand below.

Lomas follows this doubt about the possibility of scientific detachment by questioning of the desirability of the analyst's detachment from the client in the therapeutic process. He is critical of the value of the so-called 'rule of abstinence', whereby the analyst presents a blank screen to the patient. Lomas does not suggest that the analyst colludes with the patient's defences. 'If the therapist acts with wisdom he will avoid letting himself be sexually seduced by patients, recognize greed when he sees it, and resist the temptation of trying to ease his patient's pain when there is nothing active that he can do at that moment to ease it' (1987: 64). But Lomas sees no reason for therapists to abstain from answering questions or disclosing facts about themselves, and he cites examples where sharing his own feelings about the patient has been therapeutic. His concern is that the therapist should be authentic. So too 'there should be no rule to abstain from abstinence' (1987: 66) because the critique can become a dogma too.

Lomas draws upon a tradition of which glimpses are caught from time to time within the otherwise orthodox descriptions of technique. Ferenczi experimented with classical technique 'in the direction of "elasticity" and "relaxation" of Freud's more austere recommendations' (Roazen, 1979: 364). Winnicott, at least with very vulnerable patients, visited them at home, made frequent telephone calls, and took on 'a role that is more like that of a caring parent than a conventional therapist' (Lomas, 1987: 84). Furthermore, this book has already provided examples in Chapter 3 of Freud's own technique to show that he is scarcely stereotypical (Momigliano, 1987). It is unfair to hold Freud responsible for the less fortunate developments that have taken place within psychoanalysis. While Lomas is surely right to question analytic practice where it is cold, detached and aloof, what he may also be doing is to expose the difference between those who go 'by the book' and those who relate to clients with greater variety of response than is clear from their writing (see also Rowan and Jacobs, 2002, chap. 3).

Fact and Fantasy

In contrast to Guntrip's criticism that Freud sometimes believed his own speculation and turned it into fact, Freud has also come under fire for not believing the reality of actual incest and sexual abuse, treating it as fantasy (usually spelled 'phantasy' in psychoanalytic literature) rather than as fact. Particularly vehement is Masson's (1984) attempt to show that Freud suppressed his early discovery of incestuous relations because he could not tolerate isolation from the Viennese medical establishment, following their condemnation of his radical ideas. In addition, Alice Miller (1986) is only one of many writers on child abuse who also condemn Freud's retraction, and to some extent hold his subsequent theory of fantasized incestuous relations to be responsible for resistance to the acknowledgement of the prevalence of incest and abuse. Given the increasing importance paid in counselling and therapy to the reality of such traumatic experiences, it is important to examine the case against Freud.

There was clearly a shift in Freud's thinking from his early assertion that the cause of hysteria was the actual seduction of children by parents, older siblings and other family members. In 1897, when Freud wrote a letter to his friend Fliess, withdrawing support for the theory, he dropped his claim that all hysteria is caused by actual seduction. He recognized that to propose one single cause for understanding symptoms could not be right. There had to be other reasons as well. Had he been similarly qualifying any other causal explanation there would perhaps have been less criticism – he was, after all, refusing to be drawn into the type of blanket generalization, which in other instances has been one of the criticisms of his interpretations. But it appears, at least to his critics, that he totally retracted his early view. Often cited are his last words on the subject where, writing on female psychology, he uncompromisingly states:

> In the period in which the main interest was directed to discovering infantile sexual traumas, almost all of my women patients told me that they had been seduced by their father. I was driven to recognize in the end that these reports were untrue and so came to understand that hysterical symptoms are derived from phantasies and not from real occurrences. (1933a: 154)

Yet there are many other references, written at different points in his career, where Freud acknowledges the reality of actual seduction. Whatever else criticism in Vienna of his early ideas did, it did not stop him going on and developing what had been received as an outrageous theory of child development, with its emphasis on infantile sexuality. He may have written privately to Fliess in 1897, but he did not publicly withdraw his 1895 theory of actual seduction in all cases until 1903; and even then, two years later, he was publishing essays in which he clearly writes of the effect of actual seduction (1905d: 109).

He continued to believe that seduction took place, even though he believed some reported instances were the products of fantasy.

He warned that parental abuse was not that rare: 'Phantasies of being seduced are of particular interest, because so often they are not phantasies but real memories' (1916–17: 417). Freud goes on to say that such memories are not as real as they often seemed at first, and that some memories are placed in early childhood when they in fact come from later experience. What we know now about the early age at which abuse can start suggests that Freud misinterpreted some of this material. Yet he urges: 'You must not suppose, however, that sexual abuse of a child by its nearest male relatives belongs entirely to the realm of phantasy. Most analysts will have treated cases in which such events were real and could be unimpeachably established' (1916–17: 417).

These words were not published in an obscure scientific paper. They form part of the text of his public lectures, given annually over a period of years in Vienna, to lay audiences as well as to students in training. The lectures comprise one of Freud's more popular works intended for wider use. Neither then nor now do they provide any evidence of a complete retraction by Freud of the reality of abuse. If it is true, as some critics maintain, that the caring professions have understood Freud as claiming abuse to have been a figment of the imagination, the critics cannot cite in evidence Freud's words in such widely disseminated lectures as these: if anything it is the caring professionals who have ignored Freud, and who have demonstrated their own resistance, by neglecting to take note of Freud's continuing references to the widespread reality of incest and abuse. It may also be the case that Melanie Klein's much greater general emphasis on fantasy than on actual experience shifted psychoanalysis away from sufficient recognition of the external world in favour of a narrower concern for the internal world of the patient.

Freud continued to publish case material in which he clearly accepts that actual seduction has taken place. The case known as the Wolf Man (1918b/2002: 217–19) records the little boy's seduction by the elder sister. In 1924 Freud added a footnote to his case-study of Katharina (originally published in 1895, when he still believed the theory of actual seduction in all cases). In the footnote he corrects the disguise he gave her seducer, clearly believing that the incident took place: 'The girl fell ill, therefore, as a result of sexual attempts on the part of her own father' (Freud and Breuer, 1895d: 201). He reaffirms his original hypothesis. Similarly, in an essay on the psychology of women slightly earlier than the one more usually cited by his critics, he also states that 'actual seduction (by other children or someone in charge of the child) is common enough' (1931b:

379). It is difficult to believe that he could have written any of this had he held to a theory that interpreted all such reported memories as fantasies. None of these sentences provides any support for believing that he had retracted his original theory in its entirety.

The most that can be said is that Freud was inconsistent in his attitude, and perhaps ambivalent towards his early theory of actual seduction of children. The obscure hint (see p. 8) that the nursemaid, who was dismissed from his home when Freud was only two and a half years old, had been 'his teacher in sexual matters' (Gay, 1989: 7), suggests an element of personal experience of seduction. Whether this made it easier or harder for Freud to identify seduction in the stories of his patients we cannot know. Given all the references he makes to actual seduction, we need to look for a different explanation for his later phrase in the *New Introductory Lectures* that the 'reports were untrue' (1933a: 154). Its context – an essay which at best misunderstands women, and at worst, denigrates them – suggests that these lines could have been as much a gloss on the Oedipus complex in women and on hysteria as confirmation of his wish to scrap one of his earliest theories.

Feminist Critiques

The weakness of Freud's psychology of female development has been noted in Chapter 2. As in many other areas of discourse, feminist writers have drawn attention to a serious bias towards the male perspective, underplaying the particular significance of women's contribution in the arts, the part they have played in history, etc. Psychology generally comes in for similar criticism, although our purpose here is to examine the particular critique that has been made of psychoanalysis. Freud himself is muddled, and admits his lack of understanding of women – but psychoanalysis has had more than its fair share of women theorists, and it falls to them to take some of the responsibility. We must also constantly bear in mind that Freud and indeed the analysts of the first half of the twentieth century were as blinkered as those in any other discipline, yet at the same time unable to consider the arguments put forward by their own pioneers, such as Karen Horney. The reception given to her critique drove her away from the official institutes.

Freud's ideas have had a mixed reception among feminist writers: some have been deeply antagonistic towards his paternalistic attitudes and theories of women's psychology; others credit him with important and novel insights; others are critical and yet use aspects of the psychoanalytic approach.

Typical of the latter in Britain are Eichenbaum and Orbach, writing from within the women's therapy movement, which in many respects values the general psychodynamic position:

> In common with many other feminists we have several criticisms of Freud and the post-Freudian view of women's psychology. They all stem from a bias that sees female sexuality as tied to reproduction and the gratification of male impulses toward women, to women's inferiority because women and men are different, and to the control and subjugation of women. As such, the theories propose a female sexuality formed within a male image and with reference to the penis. ... The Freudian view of how women's psychology develops is fitted into a schema that sees female genitalia and femininity as inadequate and yet inevitable. The theory of female inadequacy, which is the starting point for Freudian theory on femininity, stems from his patriarchal bias. (1985: 28–9)

In the United States there are other critics of similar ilk: the feminist psychoanalytic author Dinnerstein urges against getting caught up in polemic – 'a masculine vice' (1987: 37). Feminists need to assimilate what some of the male analysts (including Freud) have seen. Although feminist critics cannot be described as speaking with the same voice, they all agree upon the necessity of taking account of the socio-economic, cultural dimension. In this, and in their general concern at the narrowness of Freud's understanding of the causes of neurosis, they share the same critique as the neo-Freudians, including the early feminist analyst Karen Horney. Although Freud acknowledged the significance of societal pressures and the restrictiveness imposed by society on individual development (see for example his outspoken criticism of men for dual standards in 1908d/2002, see page 53), his feminist critics take this much further, examining the problem of becoming and being a woman in a heavily patriarchal environment.

Typical again of a discriminating approach to Freud is Kate Millett, who values his openness about sexuality as a step towards more liberal sexual relations, but is more critical of his followers for using his writings 'to ratify traditional roles and to validate temperamental difference' (1970: 178). She further argues that women's social position has less to do with biology than with the social construction of femininity, although she is more critical in that respect of post-Freudians such as Erikson than of Freud.

Dinnerstein is similarly 'disturbed like other radical critics of our gender arrangement, by the sexual bigotry that is built into the Freudian perspective', but this does not distract her from attending to 'a way out of our gender predicament that Freud, in a sense absent-mindedly, provides. ... The conceptual tool that he put into our hands is a revolutionary one' (1987: xxiii). The revolutionary contribution Freud made was in identifying the strain put 'on male and female personality by the fates ... that the main adult presence in infancy and early childhood is female' (1987: xxiv). Freud was unable to take the step of acknowledging the major importance of the mother–child relation, because it was always the father–child relationship which received his main attention, although in his essay on *Female Sexuality* (1931b) there is, as I noted in Chapter 2, more than a hint of the crucial role played in child development by the mother (see Chapter 2, 'Gender and Female Psychology', p. 57).

What Dinnerstein does is to recognize the crucial influence of the first few years of life – indeed, the first few months of life. Although only women can bear children, it is cultural arrangements that have perpetuated the woman's almost exclusive care of (and hence power over) the child. She and Nancy Chodorow (1978, 1989, 1994) have been themselves criticized by other feminists for focusing too much on inner dynamics of the psyche and not enough on society as the primary source of women's oppression. They both say that it is family arrangements which have determined structures in society, while their critics see it the other way round, and are therefore more critical of Freud's emphasis upon individual and family dynamics.

Chodorow questions much more strongly than Dinnerstein the 'anatomy is destiny' argument suggested by Freud (1924d: 320). It is society that 'socializes particular personalities and preferences in girls and boys' (Chodorow, 1978: 25). Like Guntrip she is critical of the way Freud can slip from fantasy to reality in using such phrases as 'the discovery that she is castrated' (Freud, 1933a: 160). Psychoanalysis so often assumes 'the desirability and rightness of traditional gender roles in the family, of debilitating personality characteristics in women, and of heterosexuality, because these seem to serve functional goals of biological reproduction' (Chodorow, 1978: 155).

Chodorow follows object relations theory – which, as has been indicated, seriously questions Freud's instinctual determinism. It is relationships that matter. Drives may be manipulated and transformed in order to achieve relationships; but, she says, it is not the function of others simply to relieve the tension created by drives. She makes some clear statements about the differences between women and men: one such difference is that 'women's heterosexuality is triangular and requires a third person – a child – for its structural and emotional completion. For men, by contrast, the heterosexual relationship alone recreates the early bond to their mother; a child interrupts it' (1978: 207). In a much-quoted phrase Chodorow asserts that women's psyche is fundamentally different: 'the basic feminine sense of self is connected to the world, the basic masculine sense of self is separate' (1978: 169). She also points to gender differences in the pre-Oedipal period, earlier than Freud would place them.

While she cites research showing that fathers 'want their daughters to fit their image of a sexually attractive female person, within the limits of what is appropriate for a child' (1978: 118–19), Chodorow rejects Freud's 'shock' theory that it is because a girl finds she has no penis that she turns to father. The reason for her turning to father is that he is 'the most available person who can help her to get away from mother' (1978: 121). A boy does this more easily because he is physically different, and is treated by mother as different. A mother's 'son's maleness and oppositeness as a sexual other become important' (1978: 107); whereas pre-Oedipal mother love in girls is prolonged. Chodorow also adds to the Oedipus complex the part played by parental participation (1978: 160–3). It is not sufficient to look at the child's wishes or fantasies. Incestuous and indeed aggressive fantasies may arise earlier and more strongly in parents than in children. Chodorow has taken her examination of gender questions even further, yet from within a psychoanalytic frame, since she has, since her first book, trained as an analyst. She observes that psychoanalytic theories about women tend to generalize: indeed it is one of the criticisms that needs to be made of Freud and those who have followed him that they tend to move from the particular (their patients) to the universal. Chodorow suggests that:

> paying attention to clinical individuality and assuming that subjective gender has multiple components for everyone gives us better understanding of our patients and points us toward more accurate and complete gender theories. There are many psychologies of women. Each woman creates her own psychological gender through emotionally and conflictually charged unconscious fantasies that help construct her inner world, that projectively imbue cultural conceptions, and that interpret her sexual anatomy. By making some unconscious fantasies and interpretations more salient than others, each woman creates her own prevalent animation of gender. … We remember that any particular woman's or man's gender is a continuously invoked project in which self, identity, body imagery, sexual fantasy, fantasies about parents, cultural stories, and conflicts about intimacy, dependency, and nurturance are constructed. (1996: 215, 235)

There is therefore not one psychology of women, not even an alternative feminist psychology of women, but, as Chodorow makes clear in the title of her 1994 book, there are femininities, masculinities and sexualities. This applies as much to men, and to questions of heterosexuality and homosexuality, which, indeed, in relation to bi-sexuality Freud insisted was the case. (It should be observed in passing that although uninformed criticism is made of Freud for his attitude to homosexuality, there is no evidence whatsoever that he viewed homosexuality as pathological, and indeed considerable evidence that he fully accepted it as an alternative expression of sexuality.)

As I described in Chapter 2 ('Gender and Female Psychology', p. 57), Freud sometimes writes as if there is a difference between the psychology of men and women, and sometimes as if there is not. Feminist critiques of Freud are generally less ambivalent. Carol Gilligan's research (1982), for example, found major differences between the way men and women make moral decisions: women stress relationships, men stress rights; women are more understanding of reasons for behaviour than men, even if the behaviour itself is morally unjustifiable; and women look at the context and historical reasons that produce choices. Although Freud glimpsed this difference, he sounds like a more critical than an objective observer, when he uses phrases about women such as they 'have little sense of justice' (1933a: 168); and he is only slightly less pejorative when he writes that 'he cannot evade the notion ... that for women the level of what is ethically normal is different from what it is in men' (1925j: 342). It is difficult to avoid the impression that Freud saw women as less developed than men, genitally, emotionally and in their moral thinking. If Gilligan's work has borne out some of Freud's perceptions, she had done it without making the same value judgements.

We have to remember constantly in relation to Freud and psychoanalysis that the two are not synonymous. Psychoanalysis has now generally discarded his ideas about female sexuality. 'Freud was egregiously mistaken on this matter, and his error, unfortunately echoed by his early female disciples, has been corrected by modern psychoanalytic theorists. Those corrections are not known in some circles, and so the dead horse of Freud's outmoded notions about female psychology is still being beaten. We attribute this to poor scholarship' (Blanck and Blanck, 1994: viii–ix). A constant problem with a writer as prolific as Freud is that he is not always consistent. A phrase in one essay can often be counterbalanced by a sentence in another, quoted by friend or critic according to their point of view. While it may generally be agreed on all sides that Freud neglected the psychology of women, there is room for considerable argument about whether he was just plain wrong, or whether he was consciously or unconsciously seeking to support his patriarchal bias. He knew the weakness of his own thinking, although his ignorance might be forgiven rather more easily than some of his phraseology. What is surprising is that someone who took such pains to understand the depths of the unconscious, came so late (and perhaps too late) in life to what he believed for children was one of the most fundamental questions of all, the differences between the sexes. It has been suggested by several authors (e.g. Lehmann 1983; Orgel, 1996) that the reason for this was that he was unable to contemplate the psychology of women until after the death of his mother, which was late in his life, in 1930. It is surely not a coincidence that his essay on female sexuality was published in 1931? Or is that being too Freudian?

Cognitive-Behaviourist Critiques: Therapeutic Results

The criticisms of Freud's theories so far outlined in this chapter, whether of personality structure, of personal development or of the causes of psychological disturbance, together with the questioning of some of his techniques, frequently discriminate between what theories and practices might be useful and what might need revising in the light of further knowledge and experience. The criticism of Freud that stems from cognitive-behavioural schools of psychology is less compromising. Indeed, in some instances it seems as if the critics have cast Freud in the role of a scientific impostor, whose every idea or suggestion must be rooted out and exposed for all its falsity. It is tempting to ask why such energy has been devoted by some critics towards a man and against a theory and practice which they regard as already discredited and so obviously flawed. Eysenck is the most obvious example of this type of unrelenting crusader, who, however well reasoned in scientific argument and however critical of lack of objective evidence, has so far failed to grasp the true reasons for Freud's appeal. A similar figure although from a different perspective in the United States is Professor Frederick Crews, who pours out a stream of criticisms in 'Freud-bashing articles' (Lear, 1996: 381). Many of these criticisms would be acknowledged by modern analysts, but do not (at least in their opinion) shake the originality and creativity of a founder who is one of a number of 'revolutionary thinkers [who] have gone far beyond their data, with confirmation only coming years later, along with modification, refinement, reformulation, and partial rejection of the original model' (Michels, 1996: 575).)

The attraction of Freud's ideas and the extensive influence which his theories have had on art, literature and upon Western culture, as well as upon psychodynamic therapy and counselling, are discussed in the final chapter. It is this, perhaps, an unshakeable regard for psychoanalysis despite the lack of clear evidence for its efficacy as a healing therapy, which motivates such critics to go on campaigning against it, just as some philosophers have continued to attack religious ideas because so many have unthinkingly adhered to unprovable doctrines. But if this is the reason Eysenck and similar crusaders have chosen to undermine the widespread following which Freud has attracted, it is absolutely appropriate to give due weight to the ground which they have chosen: that of the scientific status of Freud's theories and claimed results. In these criticisms behavioural psychologists such as Eysenck are joined by cognitive therapists such as Ellis.

The first major criticism, and perhaps in practice the most important, is that the therapeutic effects of psychotherapy (in this context, of the psychodynamic and non-directive type) are either small or are non-existent. In a sequence of papers over a number of years, but particularly in the first (1952), Eysenck attacked the effectiveness of psychoanalytic therapy 'which he regards as worse than useless – in fact definitely deleterious to a patient's well-being' (Kline, 1981: 391). Eysenck claimed that 70 per cent of neurotic disorders improved without treatment, a figure based on previous research, and used in the absence of a control group. He argued that therapists needed to show a significantly higher success rate than 70 per cent to claim success. He went on to compile his own figures for the success of psychoanalytic therapy, using five studies and a total sample of 760 cases. Here he calculated a 44 per cent success rate, although a rather different method of calculation produced a figure of 66 per cent. His conclusions were that psychoanalytic therapy was not successful, and could even be positively harmful (Eysenck, 1952).

The paper raised a storm of protest. 'This brief, factual and innocuous paper produced a whole shower of replies, critiques, refutations, arguments and discussions; it did not, however, produce a single mention of a single experiment or clinical trial which had demonstrated a positive effect for psychoanalytic treatment' (Eysenck, 1963: 71). Nevertheless, several psychologists have since challenged Eysenck's data for the quantification of the outcome of psychoanalytic therapy, and his concept of spontaneous remission

(Kline, 1981: 392–3). For example, he claimed to use 484 cases from one paper, when the true figure was 604. Kline (a professor of psychometrics) summarizes the conclusions that follow from Eysenck's paper: 'the base rate of spontaneous remission so ingeniously derived by Eysenck is by no means so clear-cut as he would have us believe. ... The criterion for recovery is so different from school to school of psychotherapy that comparison is not meaningful' (1981: 393). Eysenck later claimed (1965) that he had deliberately overstated the case to provoke research – a curious way of demonstrating his concern for scientific accuracy.

Freud had in his own lifetime countered the advice to produce statistical evidence of psychoanalytic successes, by arguing, firstly that statistics are valueless if cases are not equivalent; secondly that time is too short to judge the permanence of cures; and thirdly by saying that many patients want to keep their therapy secret. 'The strongest reason for holding back lay in the realization that in matters of therapy, people behave highly irrationally, so that one has no prospect of accomplishing anything with them by rational means' (Freud, 1916–17: 515). Rachman and Wilson do not believe Freud's objections are valid, except the problem of comparing like with like, although they agree that 'major problems remain and those of assessing the effects of therapy in a valid manner are among the most taxing' (1980: 51).

Research into the efficacy of many types of therapy and counselling is now taking place on a scale significantly larger than anything that the early researchers and critics of psychoanalysis pioneered. Psychoanalysis responded to earlier criticism in a number of studies, such as Malan's study (1963) of brief therapy at the Tavistock Clinic in London. Rachman and Wilson comment on the integrity of Malan's work, and 'his exceptional readiness to ask hard and even painful questions' (1980: 65). Malan himself has said that outcome studies 'have almost entirely failed to provide evidence favourable to psychotherapy' (1963: 151). But Rachman and Wilson are nevertheless critical of some aspects of Malan's research and conclude that out of three major studies at the time (Malan, the Menninger Report and the Sloane study), only the last yields satisfactory results. The others do not provide a basis for reaching any conclusions, whether positive or negative (1980: 75). When they were writing in 1980 Rachman and Wilson said that those who had made serious attempts to research into outcome (from within psychoanalysis) had concluded that the figures do not, to quote one report, 'prove analytic therapy to be effective or ineffective' (Rachman and Wilson, 1980: 58).

Writing around the same time Kline examined many of the researches into Freudian theories, and noted that the evidence for the therapeutic effect of psychoanalytic therapy 'leaves much to be desired' (1981: 406). He pointed out that various studies (such as those by Malan) had developed criteria for the measurement of psychoanalytic therapy. But Kline was clearly disturbed that analysts largely refuse to allow any objective observation (through tapes or cameras) of the psychoanalytic session itself. At the time of writing, some twenty years on, that refusal remains largely the case, although it is also important to note that Peter Fonagy, Freud Memorial Professor at University College London, is one of the authors of a comprehensive review of research into many types of therapy – *What Works for Whom?* (Roth and Fonagy, 1996). Writing in the *International Journal of Psycho-Analysis*, Emde and Fonagy observe that psychoanalysis grew largely in isolation from universities, and focused on only one method of enquiry, the psychoanalytic situation (1997: 643) and that most psychoanalysts are trained as 'practitioners, not academicians, nor are they in a position to devote the majority of their time to research' (1997: 650). The article describes the development of a research training programme for practitioners, and looks forward to an emerging psychoanalytic culture that aids research.

The necessity of research, partly to win funding for the employment of particular approaches and applications of counselling and psychotherapy, means that this is a burgeoning field of study, affecting psychodynamic work, which might be called applied psychoanalysis, adapted to once-weekly work and to brief therapy as well. The results of research are coming on stream so fast that any summary here would be superseded before long, so I do not propose to enter this fascinating arena, except to observe that there appears to be increasing evidence of the effectiveness of many different approaches to therapy and counselling, including the psychodynamic and person-centred therapies that Eysenck originally questioned. It must be remembered that if there is, at the time of publication of this second edition, little evidence yet of the effectiveness of long-term psychoanalysis, this is because it has not yet been researched, and by definition will take much longer than research into time-limited therapies. Furthermore, the promotion of reflective practice as one means of research restores the psychoanalytic method to a proper place in research. We may await results with interest.

Ironically, although Freud argued that it was impossible to convince sceptics of the efficacy of his technique, he also anticipated that the day might come when psychoanalysis would be superseded by drugs as a method of treatment of neurotic disorders. 'Given the close connections between things that we divide into physical and mental, it is predictable that the day will come when paths of cognition and also, hopefully, of influence, will open up the biological study of the organs and chemistry, and the territory of the phenomena of neurosis' (1926e/2002: 140).

Is Psychoanalysis a Science?

A major criticism of psychoanalysis by cognitive and behavioural psychologists has been its apparent lack of a research method and base. The nature of scientific enquiry, and the value of qualitative as well as quantitative research have rendered some of this debate dated. As Emde and Fonagy point out, '"post-modernistic" twentieth-century science has taught us that all fields of observation are influenced by the method of observation and the observer' and that 'meaning is profoundly influenced by personal, historical and cultural contexts' (1997: 643). Therapists have argued among themselves whether their field is an art or a science, although Freud himself seems to have had no doubt that psychoanalysis was a science, but his notion of science is not the same as the notion of science today. Therefore the old debate as to whether Freudian theory is indeed scientific, which has been raised by many critics (notably Eysenck, 1953; Popper, 1959) as well as by others who are more sympathetic to psychoanalysis, may also not be as important as once it was, since the psychoanalytic method of enquiry has a different kind of validity.

Yet while this widening approach to research may alter or validate some psychoanalytic technique, there remains the question of Freud's theories of the psyche and psychopathology. Here the old arguments about how scientific his ideas are still apply: for a theory to be scientific it needs to be based upon observations, which as far as possible are made under controlled conditions, in order to limit the influence of external variables. A scientific theory must use clearly specified and identifiable concepts; and it must present hypotheses that are capable of being tested through replicated experiments or observations. Popper further argues that to be scientific a statement also needs to be refutable. It must not only be capable of being shown to be correct; it must also be capable of being proved wrong. For example, the statement that the back of the moon is made of cheese is a scientific hypothesis (Kline, 1981: 2). Even before the time that observations could be made of the back of the moon it was nevertheless possible *in principle* to test and refute such a statement. Since the advent of space exploration we know that this hypothesis has been proved wrong, but it remains a (dated) scientific hypothesis. However, it will never be possible to test or refute the Freudian claim that there are two instinctual forces in humans, the life instinct and the death instinct.

There are other theories, including very fundamental aspects in Freud's writings – many of his strictest critics would say virtually all of them – that are not capable of fulfilling these requirements, and therefore cannot on this basis be called scientific hypotheses. They are philosophical statements rather than scientific ones (often called metapsychology, in the same way as theological statements have been called metaphysics); or they are based upon limited observations. Much of Freud's original thinking was built upon what he heard, saw and speculated upon during therapy. Nearly all the data upon which psychoanalytic theory is therefore based comes from clients' own reporting, and cannot usually be validated by an independent person. It is rarely recorded in detail at the time, and it is not compared with information coming from a control group, even if it were possible to set up such a group. Many of the hypotheses put forward by Freud are therefore exceedingly difficult to test; although this does not necessarily prove all Freud's ideas to be wrong, the sceptic is unlikely to be impressed.

Kline admits that psychoanalytic theory is open to serious criticism. However, he suggests that the 'theory is of such a kind that these criticisms are not necessarily entirely destructive' (1981: 2). In the first instance, some aspects of psychoanalytic theory are testable: some of Freud's observations can be examined to see whether they are true, even if it is not always possible to test Freud's explanations of his observations. For example, it is possible to test whether the Oedipal stage as described by Freud has any validity – that boys (or girls) at the phallic stage of development have an overt love for their mothers (or fathers) and that later this is repressed. However, it is impossible to test scientifically Freud's claim that the Oedipal situation contains a genetic element in it – a trace memory passed down through the genes from the 'primal horde', where Freud speculated (without any evidence) that the young men in the prehistoric tribe killed the dominant male. In fact, modern studies of genetics indicate that the inheritance of acquired characteristics is not possible, rendering the theory even more implausible. Other Freudian explanations fall outside the area of testability, and fully justify the description which psychoanalysis already gives them of being in the realm of metapsychology.

Theological or other metaphysical statements such as aesthetics are similarly incapable of proof or refutation. But since Freud claimed scientific status for so many of his theories, the possibility of challenging them on scientific grounds has naturally been examined and in some instances been found wanting.

Psychoanalytic thought, however, does not have to be seen as a unified theory, which stands or falls by each single part of it. Some psychoanalytic hypotheses may be shown to be false, without this necessarily undermining other parts of Freudian thinking. Freud's metapsychology may be unscientific, but some of the implicit empirical propositions that can be tested are not; and if some of those empirical propositions are proved to be false, others may find sufficient support.

Nevertheless, when Freudian propositions are tested, we have to be careful about how we interpret results. Both positive and negative results may be the result of faulty research design, or of faulty execution of the design. Kline (1981) has examined a large number of experiments and sets of observations, and considers the following to be important before the results of any test can put Freudian propositions on to a scientific basis: first, there has to be a sampling procedure, and use of control groups; secondly, a test has to have proven validity; thirdly, the statistical analysis of results has to be significant; and finally, an experiment has to be relevant to psychoanalytic theory or another possible hypothesis. Even then, as Kline points out, there may be other explanations of results than those offered by the researcher. He quotes a light piece of research in which significantly more men than women returned their pencils following an exam. Although this could be explained as evidence of penis envy, 'it could, of course, also indicate that women need pencils more than men or are more dishonest than men or more flustered by the rigours of examination' (1981: 153).

To some extent Freud tried to counter and anticipate the arguments that might be adduced from research into the effectiveness of his methods, although he was clearly unable to anticipate some of the research into his theoretical base. He was obviously sensitive to the charge that psychoanalysis was not a science, and gave his own answer to those who contemptuously felt unable to take his ideas seriously. In his autobiography he recognized that it was often said that psychoanalysis was not a science because its concepts lacked precision. In reply he wrote that 'clear fundamental concepts and sharply drawn definitions are only possible in the mental sciences in so far as the latter seek to fit a department of facts into the frame of a logical system' (1925d: 242). He went on to draw the parallel with zoology or botany as unable at first to give correct definitions of an animal or plant; and even at the time he wrote that biology was 'unable to give any certain meaning to the concept of life' (1925d: 242). He accepted that his science was incomplete and insufficient, and that it had 'to work out its findings piecemeal and to solve its problems step by step' (1925d: 242), because it had no alternative method for doing this other than through observation.

It is important to remember that Freud was no stranger to the scientific method of enquiry. He was well used to the experimental method in his initial posts in neurology, and his papers in that particular scientific field were extremely well received. Yet he proposed no large-scale testing of his psychological hypotheses. His original hypotheses were made on the basis of observation (not an uncommon scientific method), but confirmation could only come through subsequent observations. Despite Freud's awareness of criticism and his frequent references to the need to test the evidence and to throw out what was unsound, there remained (and remains) a particular danger in his method of enquiry, which relied (and relies) so heavily upon observation. Having formed an initial hypothesis, Freud and his followers could as easily interpret later patients' material as confirmation of the original hypotheses, rather than consider alternative explanations. There is some evidence that Freud himself did this. Speaking at the end of his life, a former patient, known as the Wolf Man, recalled aspects of his treatment with Freud:

> When he [Freud] had explained everything to me, I said to him, 'All right then, I agree, but I am going to check whether it is correct.' And he said: 'Don't start that. Because the moment you try to view things critically, your treatment will get nowhere. I will help you, whether you now believe in it, or not.' So I naturally gave up the idea of any further criticism. (Obholzer, 1980: 31)

Perhaps, to put a positive gloss on this incident, Freud was trying to encourage the Wolf Man away from intellectualization. But there is also evidence of Freud forcing meanings on to the patient: 'In my story, what was explained by dreams? Nothing as far as I can see. Freud traces everything back to the primal scene which he derives from the dream. But that scene does not occur in the dream. It's terribly far-fetched' (Obholzer, 1980: 35).

Freud was not the first, and will not be the last, to be convinced and carried away at times by the apparent neatness of his theories. Other scientists, including some psychologists, have done the same. As Michels observes, 'Freud was a creative and innovative thinker, but ... he was not an elegant scientific methodologist' (1996: 575), and if Crews singles out, as he does in *The Memory Wars* (1995) 'one specific and important methodological problem, the contamination of clinical psychoanalytic data by suggestion ... suggestion is universal in all psychotherapeutic treatment, and, indeed, in almost all medical treatment. What is unique about psychoanalysis, of course, is not the presence of suggestion, but rather the recognition of its presence, the attempt to explore it, to understand its basis, and to minimize its influence' (Michels 1996: 575).

Researching Freudian Theory

A useful summary of various research studies into different aspects of Freud's theories has been set out by Kline (1981). As much as possible he draws upon studies where the methodology was sound, and he concentrates upon those hypotheses put forward by Freud which are capable of being tested. For example, the three main hypotheses in the Freudian theory of psychosexual development are:

1   that there are personality types in mature adults;
2   that these are related to the child's experiences that result from particular ways of child-rearing;
3   that the mouth, anus and phallus are erotogenic zones in early childhood.

When all the studies known to Kline at that time are considered, the evidence appears to suggest that there is strong support for what Freudians call 'anal' character, reasonable support for the 'oral' character, but no evidence in favour of other psychosexual syndromes. As to the origins of such psychological characteristics through specific child-rearing practices, Freudian theory about the relationship between weaning and oral characteristics, and anal characteristics and anal erotism, is only supported by a few studies. Oral erotism is confirmed but its link with personality is not. Other studies suggest more common-sense explanations – such as orderly parents tending to produce orderly children, and these tend to provide more support for neo-Freudian and some post-Freudian thinking, that it is the relationship between parents and child that produces attitudes to oral and anal pleasure, rather than the handling of erotogenic zones which gives rise to the child's developing character.

Despite the heavy weight of negative evidence about Freudian psychosexual development in infancy, Kline says that there are profound difficulties involved in testing psychological hypotheses involving infants. Methodological problems are more than enough to account for the failures of many studies to support Freudian psychosexual theory.

Kline similarly examines research into other Freudian concepts, first by isolating key hypotheses, and then listing the studies to show whether there is strong or weak support, or no evidence at all, for many of the central ideas put forward by Freud. For example, there is some confirmation of the Oedipus complex, although Kline suggests that Freud attaches too much importance to it. However, another aspect of the Oedipal stage, castration anxiety, is impressively supported. There is some evidence for three types of mental activity that are characteristic of the id, ego and super-ego, although here it is process rather than structure that seems to be supported. Repression, as the most important of Freud's defence mechanisms, is powerfully supported, even though some other defences have not been confirmed to the same degree. Kline observes that one particular defence called 'reaction-formation' has done psychoanalysis a disservice. It is a good example of that upside-down Freudian thinking which appears from time to time, where a particular feeling is 'proved' to be present, even if the opposite appears to be the case. This spurious argument might run: extreme messiness is a sign of anal character; but where you find extreme tidiness it is obviously a sign of reaction against messiness, thus still indicating an anal character!

Sexual symbolism is well supported within and outside dreams, suggesting that psychoanalytic theories about art and literature as expressions of sexual sublimation may have some value. The importance of dreams and their sexual content has been verified, although research suggests that greater importance needs to be attached to the manifest (obvious) content than Freud allowed. There is also support for some of the theories put forward by Freud about the underlying reasons for certain mental disturbances, such as the homosexual element in paranoia, and the aetiology of anorexia and of depression.

I am aware that in these paragraphs, I select, abbreviate and summarize the summaries of research studies that Kline makes in his examination of the validity of Freudian concepts. The information available here to the reader is at least two removes from the original research. This in itself signals a warning about attempts to confirm or refute Freudian theory on the basis of second-hand information. Those interested in research, and who have a mind for statistics and questions of methodology, may find Kline's study of interest. It is, of course, itself a pointer to extensive literature.

The Status of Psychoanalytic Discourse

Others, particularly those who prefer to see therapy as more of an art than a science and more a set of interpersonal skills than a quasi-medical method of treatment, may wonder how to use such an array of information as emerges from these research studies. They clearly have bearing on theoretical formulations, and theory provides background information for therapy itself. Yet therapy itself is about much more than theories of psychological structure or psychosocial development. Are such 'scientific' questions particularly relevant to the counselling session or to the therapeutic relationship?

In what I believe (and the term 'believe' betrays my own less than scientific approach) to be the most effective therapy sessions, the actual language used and the level of insight achieved by therapist and client is very rarely phrased in the terminology that Freud and his followers used to describe and explain the workings of the human mind. The functions described for id, ego and super-ego may find some backing in research, and indeed make sense of our subjective experience of the way our minds work; but they are terms that are unlikely to be used in the conversation between therapist and client. Some of Freud's concepts have entered common parlance: 'neurosis', 'projection', even 'the Oedipus complex'. But even when such terms are understood by the client they are not part of the normal verbal interchange between the psychodynamically orientated therapist and her or his client. Explanations and interpretations are best couched in the language and using the concepts that make sense to the particular client. In clinical practice, theoretical formulations have their use in supervision and in communications between therapists, and in providing a kind of 'map' for the counsellor or therapist who seeks to understand the disorientations of the client's experience.

Kline emphasizes that it may be more valuable to approach Freud's work as consisting of a large number of theories, rather than as a unified whole. Some of what Freud has tried to identify has proved useful, some has not, and some remains unproven, although worth thinking about further. Therapists who work with a cross-section of clients (in other words, who are not in a position to select or attract clients who seem to suit their own theory and practice) find that aspects of Freud's work appear at different times with different clients; but so too do aspects of Jungian, Kleinian or object relations therapy.

The studies assembled by Kline are valuable in indicating the caution that is necessary about universalizing single Freudian concepts. They may apply to some people some of the time, but not to everyone all of the time. Freud himself recognized the dangers of doing this. On one occasion he commented on a paper given in his presence: 'This is the kind of paper that will bring psychoanalysis into disrepute. You cannot reduce everything to the Oedipus complex. Stop!' (Kardiner, 1958: 50).

What emerges from these studies is the question of how research results are to be interpreted. However valuable accurate statistics and however crucial correct methodology, in the end the impression is sometimes given that even those who seek to be scientific and objective have a wish for certain outcomes. As I indicated at the start of this chapter, Freud's work stresses the powerful influence that the unconscious can have over conscious rationality, and puts a further question mark over the possibility of objectivity, which of course twentieth-century scientific method has also recognized.

It may be, of course, that the scientific method is not the best way of approaching, understanding or applying criticism to Freudian theory. Some suggest that Freudian theory is on a different plane to scientific theory. Ricoeur (1970) argues that what is important to psychoanalytic theory is the way in which environmental variables appear to the subject, not the observer. Scientifically verifiable quantification cannot deal with the subjective meanings that people attach to their experiences, and it is the meanings that people give to experience that form the essential part of psychoanalysis. Gill (1991) has also argued that psychoanalysis is 'a hermeneutic science – hermeneutic because it interprets meanings, scientific because the meaning connections it deals with are also usually causal connections' (Brook, 1995: 519).

If this is the case it is not surprising that many of the experiments testing Freudian theory are bound to produce negative results. It is a familiar experience in therapy to hear a client say 'I know this is silly, but I think ...' Some people questioned in surveys do not necessarily give the answer they feel (in case it is 'silly'), but the answer they think they are expected to give. Furthermore, some of the anxieties or fantasies that people have are 'unconscious' – or at least so Freudian theory maintains. It is because they are unconscious that such fantasies have influence and power. We would not expect such unconscious meanings to emerge from questions alone. Freud soon discovered this when he abandoned asking questions, and turned to free association as a more productive method. Asked questions, people give answers that are capable of different interpretations, depending upon the interpreter's point of view. Kline cites an experiment into castration anxiety (1981: 149–50), where it was found that there was no hint among the sample of 190 boys and girls aged about five years old of the fantasy that little girls had been castrated. Similarly, 95 per cent of these children said that birth through the anus was an impossibility. Asked such questions, it is not surprising that such rational answers were given. It is similarly much more difficult to get access to those thoughts and fantasies that children imagine an adult would think were 'silly'.

It is clear that Freud's early postgraduate researches into neurology were good examples of natural science, and were both meticulous and original. He naturally took this scientific approach into his psychological researches. His observations in this new field remained just as meticulous and original. Looking back on his work, the particular interpretations that arose from those observations exhibit a subtle shift, from what he imagined was still a strictly scientific discipline, to one which was a pot-pourri of philosophy of mind and persons, of metaphor, myth and metapsychology. Despite this shift he continued to try to use scientific methods in formulating a psychopathology of neuroses. Although Freud dearly wished for his theories to be accepted as part of scientific research, much is lost if they are only regarded as such. Scientific discourse tends to lead to black and white distinctions: one theory is supported, another hypothesis is disconfirmed. To make such clear distinctions with Freud's ideas is to risk losing opportunities for insight that come not through scientific proof, but through empathic awareness of the problems of human existence that he struggled to understand. The next chapter makes it clear that Freud's psychoanalysis stands as a discourse in its own right alongside the social sciences, and literary and historical criticism. Freud's mistake was to lay such stress on the scientific status of his quest for truth.

He found it difficult, of course, to write in any other way. He wished to place his theories within the scientific tradition. Yet there was also that about him that could not be contained within one discipline, which spilled over into areas less capable of being understood through scientific observation alone. This is most obvious in his writing about anthropology and religion, but it is also present at the many points when he tries to contain and explain what even now still have to be called 'mysteries' of the human mind. His enthusiasm for this task is revealed in the recollection that 'in my youth I developed an overwhelming desire to understand some of the mysteries of this world and perhaps to contribute something towards solving them' (Freud, 1927a/2002: 165). In his seventies he looked back: 'After forty-one years of activity as a doctor, my self-knowledge told me I had not actually been a proper doctor. I became a doctor through being deflected against my will from my original intention, and the great triumph of my life is that after a long detour I found my initial direction again' (1927a/2002: 165).

That it is right to place Freud within a wider context than just the scientific, and to see him as much as the artist who interprets as the scientist who explains, becomes even more obvious in the final chapter where Freud's overall influence is assessed. Whatever shortcomings there are in the theory and the practice Freud gave us, elements of both his theory and his practice have penetrated deeply into our culture. While it is highly dangerous to equate the popularity of any set of beliefs with their truth, the interest aroused by his ideas in so many intellectual fields is a mark of the seriousness with which he must be taken.

5

Freud's Influence on Therapy
and the Wider World

> if he was often wrong and at times, absurd,
> to us he is no more a person
> now but a whole climate of opinion
> under whom we conduct our different lives

> W.H. Auden: 'In Memory of Sigmund Freud'

Assessing Freud

Writers and their subjects, children and parents, disciples and their master, long-term clients and their therapists, and patients and their analysts, may have something in common: they usually spend months or even years with each other, and in some sense psychologically inside each other; and they build up that almost inevitable love–hate relationship that comes from such a long and close attachment. While on the one hand this relationship probably leads to intimate knowledge, it also leads, to a varying extent, to some loss of objectivity. It may be difficult to see the other in their wider context. Attention has already been drawn to examples where Freud, perhaps because of his own familiarity with some of his speculations, converted them into quasi facts.

Freudian therapists and analysts, many of whom spend years absorbing the work of their master, and who experience his indirect influence on them through their personal therapy, may at times find it difficult to achieve the necessary distance for unbiased reflection on the theoretical base of their training. Lomas recalls that Winnicott suggested that no analyst should depart from recommended technique until he had ten years' experience of routine practice behind him. Lomas sees it very differently: 'It takes ten years for most psychoanalysts to gain the confidence to depart from a technical approach which they should never have adopted in the first place' (1973: 147). As I now set out to examine Freud's influence I too am aware that having read, written about and at times almost lived Freud, the temptation is to eulogize rather than assess, to deify rather than discriminate. I have already noted Kernberg's criticism of psychoanalytic education and its tendency to idealize Freud (p. 103). Since many of those who write about Freud's influence, and who do so from the vantage point of a thorough study of the history of modern thought and culture, similarly describe him in magisterial terms it is difficult to avoid the charge of idealization even in quoting them. For every negative voice, such as Eysenck's or Crews', there are a dozen more who positively assess Freud's contribution to twentieth-century thought not only as powerful but also as profound.

Eysenck himself recognizes, although with what seems like some incredulity and a little pique, that 'psychoanalysis is almost the only type of psychology at all well known; indeed to most people, psychoanalysis *is* psychology' (1963: 66). He goes on to equate Freud and his followers with a group of 'prophets rather than scientists' (1963: 67). Rieff, using Eysenck's same term, assesses Freud's position quite differently: 'No prophet of our destiny, neither Marx nor Darwin or any other has spoken with greater import to the human condition' (1959). Eysenck criticizes Freud's ideas as 'heresies' (1963: 66), describing them disparagingly as being on a par with religious statements (1963: 68). In contrast, Kazin, in a somewhat sweeping statement but one which contains some truth, suggests that 'psychoanalytical literature has replaced the Bible as the place to which people turn for an explanation of their suffering and a source of consolation' (1958: 15); and Rieff's assessment is that Freud 'will not help those who suffer from residual beliefs to find new beliefs; he can only help us in our unbelief' (1973: 33). Again, Eysenck entitles one of his critical essays 'Psychoanalysis – myth or science' (1963: 66–81). Using the same concept but more positively, the novelist D.M. Thomas, in the Preface to his novel *The White Hotel*, describes Freud as the 'discoverer of the great and beautiful modern myth of psychoanalysis' (1981: 6). Myth, used in this positive sense, aptly describes the search for meaning behind the whole corpus of psychoanalytic theory. We might use the idea of metaphor and symbolization to show the type of imaginative truth that might lie behind many of Freud's more specific concepts and 'scientific' constructs. In using the term 'myth', Thomas says that he does 'not intend to put into question the scientific validity of psychoanalysis' but he prefers to emphasize psychoanalysis as a 'poetic, hidden expression of a hidden truth' (1981: 6).

Whether or not such positive assessments of Freud's work as these are in the end proved right, it cannot be refuted that Freud's work made an enormous impact on twentieth-century Western culture, both at an intellectual and at a popular level, and that this influence extends into the present time. It is perhaps significant that the whole of the Standard Edition was published in paperback in 2001, and that the new translations of Freud in Penguin Classics were published from 2002 onwards. His writing is as alive as it has ever been. Even the arch-critic Eysenck states that psychoanalysis has become the leading school in psychiatry in many countries, and that it is well known 'among novelists, film makers, journalists, teachers, philosophers, and even among the general public' (1963: 66).

If it has been difficult to convey an adequate picture of Freud's life and work in the previous four chapters, it is an even harder task to describe his overall influence in this final one. This is made so because Freud's influence cannot be confined to therapy and counselling. Although I naturally give priority to the influence of Freud on the development of theory and to his continuing influence upon practice, especially within psychoanalytic and psychodynamic schools, to give adequate attention to the effects of Freud's thinking I have also to discuss, albeit briefly, the fact that many of his ideas have been taken up by schools of philosophy, literary criticism, history, theology and sociology, as well as in the whole artistic and literary enterprise in Western culture. In the vacuum created by the decline of religious belief and consequently of Christian culture, it is a somewhat exaggerated claim to describe, as Badcock does, the psychoanalytic revolution as going far beyond the Renaissance: 'Psychoanalysis, in doing what Catholicism did, but in doing it so much more completely and effectively, will ... produce a general renaissance of culture' (1980: 253). Badcock tends to idealize Freud, but the sentiment is understandable.

These different areas of influence, within the field of therapy and counselling, and in the wider cultural field itself, are evidence of the interrelatedness between psychoanalysis, science and the arts that Freud so cherished. He clearly wished that psychoanalysis should be applied more widely in other disciplines as well as in medicine. Not only did he consider it necessary that analytic training should include 'cultural history, mythology, the psychology of religion and literary studies' (1926e/2002: 154); he also asserted in several places that psychoanalysis, as a theory of the unconscious, would 'become indispensable to all the branches of knowledge which are to do with the history of the rise of human culture and its great institutions such as art, religion and the social order' (1926e/2002: 156). Similarly, in his autobiography Freud maintained that psychoanalysis is as important in the field of education as it is in medicine (1925d: 259).

Developments in Psychoanalysis

I have already made reference to some of the developments that have stemmed from Freud, in summarizing in Chapter 4 some of his critics, critics who have built upon some of his ideas, while at the same time observing the narrowness of certain aspects of Freudian theory. Freud's influence upon psychoanalysis is so extensive it is difficult not to stray into the ideas of those who have to some extent taken the lead in the developments of psychoanalysis. But at the risk of exaggerating the impact of his work on all therapy, attention must first be drawn to those outside the psychoanalytic movement who started within it, but distanced themselves from it. Their own unique contributions must in no way be minimized, especially since they were often correcting what was missing or over-emphasized within the Freudian schema of theory or practice. Yet Freud's influence can be seen in them all.

Reference has been made in Chapter 4 to Adler and Jung, who split from Freud when the psychoanalytic movement was still in its infancy. Others have been alluded to, such as the neo-Freudians, who gradually moved away from mainstream psychoanalysis in the decade after Freud's death. There are many others who started within psychoanalysis, also key figures in therapy and counselling, some of whom form the subject of other volumes in this series: Fritz Perls and Gestalt therapy (Clarkson and Mackewn, 1993), Wilhelm Reich and orgone therapy, leading in turn to bio-energetics, Albert Ellis and rational-emotive therapy (Yankura and Dryden, 1994), Eric Berne and Transactional Analysis (Stewart, 1992), and even Carl Rogers and person-centred therapy (Thorne, 2003). Sometimes these therapists developed their own methods and theoretical framework as a reaction to Freudian theory or practice, although in some instances they were reacting against institutionalized psychoanalysis, as they experienced it, since the organization was unable to accommodate their own pioneering work.

Orthodox psychoanalysis has a turbulent and consequently confusing history, with different groups within it influenced by various aspects of Freud's theory. The following sections simply point to the rich and diverse development of Freud's work, which from a different perspective has at times looked more like a series of family feuds. The different emphases given by the factions within psychoanalysis often owe much to Freud's original thoughts. In turn the different emphases within the psychoanalytic movement have influenced psychodynamic therapy and counselling in general. Fortunately, the ethos of most training courses, and the setting of many practices in counselling and less intensive psychotherapy, have encouraged a form of psychodynamic integration, which is able to draw upon what seems most relevant in the different psychoanalytic schools, both for the particular therapist and the particular client.

Ego-Psychology

Freud's growing interest in the place of the ego within the structure of personality has particularly influenced (as one might expect) the work of his daughter Anna Freud in Britain (1936), and Heinz Hartmann (1939) and others such as Kris, Jacobson, Spitz, Mahler, Kernberg and to some extent Kohut in the United States, with their emphasis on 'ego-psychology', or, in the last-named case, what has become known as 'self psychology' (see Blanck and Blanck, 1994). It is Freud's drive/structural model that has proved fruitful ground for further understanding of the 'ego'. Anna Freud added particularly to Freud's definitions of mechanisms of defence (1936), showing a deeper appreciation of the actual relationship between a child and her or his mother. The effect on the child of the outside world, particularly that of adults in her or his immediate environment, is understood in ego-psychology to influence development more significantly than perhaps Freud, and certainly Melanie Klein, appreciated.

In the United States Freud's influence on mainstream psychoanalysis has been much stronger than in Britain, where the Freudian school has had to compete with the Kleinian on the one hand, or a middle group on the other. Hartmann in America argued strongly against the culturalist school of Fromm, Horney, Thompson and Sullivan, accusing them of simplifying and abbreviating the complex structure of Freud's thinking; although he also attempted to encompass their insights into the framework of Freud's drive model. This integrative stance is also found in other Freudian drive theorists such as Margaret Mahler (and her work on separation/individuation) and Edith Jacobson (and her writing on the 'self', 1964), although they have a more fully developed view of the internal world of object relations than Freud ever had. Hartmann, Mahler and Jacobson in turn have influenced certain aspects of Otto Kernberg's theory (1976, 1980), showing how Freud's ideas have passed through a series of adaptations, but continue to influence succeeding generations of analysts. Kernberg 'positions himself within the evolving tradition of the drive/structural model' although he is also 'the only American psychoanalyst to characterize his work as an "object relations theory"' (Greenberg and Mitchell, 1983: 327).

The Kleinian School

Melanie Klein, like Anna Freud, modified Freud's technique so that she could work better with children (Klein, 1932). Using play and other substitutes for the purely verbal she believed that she could gain access to the unconscious of young children. The material that she gathered from children's fantasies (which again she prefers to spell as 'phantasies') stressed themes of sadism, anxiety and guilt. Klein was herself strongly influenced by Freud's theory of the death drive, which she adopted, according to Guntrip, 'in the most uncompromising way' (1961: 198). Guntrip does not believe her theory of aggression is truly an instinctual one, despite Melanie Klein and her associates hanging on to Freud's instinct theory 'with grim tenacity' (1961: 208).

Guntrip in fact assesses Klein's contribution as moving away from the psychobiological and the instinct theory towards psychodynamic concepts (1961: 207). But she took Freud's concept of the super-ego and extended it to other persecutory parental images, 'an explanation which developed in course of time into the theory of internal objects' (Guntrip, 1961: 197). She also took hold of Freud's concepts of the super-ego and the Oedipus complex, but placed their origins earlier, in the first two years of infancy.

In the development of both her practice and her theory Melanie Klein was supported by one of Freud's close colleagues and eventual biographer, Ernest Jones. He was himself critical of Freud in some respects, particularly over female psychological development. It was he who invited Klein to London, where she settled in 1926. Freud himself 'abhorred the direction Melanie Klein took' although he was 'moderate in his public pronouncements' about her (Roazen, 1979: 473). For her part Melanie Klein and her followers saw themselves as the true heirs of Freud. They are known, somewhat ironically given her European origins, as the English school.

The Kleinians on the one side and the supporters of Anna Freud on the other, both claimed directly to extend Freud's theories, particularly in the euphemistically named 'Scientific Controversies' that took place in London during the time of the Second World War. This minor war between two factions, that at times became very bitter, is meticulously recorded in *The Freud–Klein Controversies 1941–45* (King and Steiner, 1991). What began in the 1920s as a disagreement between Klein and Anna Freud over technique in child analysis, expanded into a major ideological schism. Greenberg and Mitchell, whose book on the variants of object relations theory is a valuable summary of key post-Freudian thinkers, assert that Klein has been 'denounced by many psycho-analytic authors for distorting and betraying basic principles of sound psychoanalytic theory and practice' (1983: 120). They assess her as both remaining true to as well as departing from Freud's vision, making her a key transitional figure between instinct theory and object relations. Guntrip emphasizes that what some think to be a '"deviation" from Freud consists, in fact, of the radical development of Freud's own greatest deviation from himself' (1961: 207).

Both sets of followers of Freud in Britain have been involved over many years in an internecine battle which at times has threatened to tear apart the British psychoanalytic movement, as well as split the international psychoanalytic community. In the United States Melanie Klein's influence is far less pronounced, although there has been more interest in representatives of a third, 'middle group', consisting largely of those, like Winnicott, who were unwilling to choose either side, aligning themselves with what is known as object relations theory, but again acknowledging the importance to them of Freud's original studies.

Object Relations Theory

Melanie Klein's work, whatever reservations some may have about it, saw the start of a more clearly defined object relations theory, with significant contributions from Fairbairn (1952), Winnicott (1958) and Guntrip (1961, 1968). Freud's influence on the development of object relations theory is direct and is not just permeated through Melanie Klein, as shown in Chapter 2 where aspects of Freud's theories can be seen that set down markers for the development of object relations theory. All four major contributors to British psychoanalytic theory make plain their relationship to Freud's work. It is his influence on them that I particularly consider here.

Although Klein clearly pioneered her own techniques in child analysis, Winnicott (Jacobs, 1995) developed his own style of more intensive work with deeply regressed patients, and in his work with children, perhaps taking Freud as his mentor more than Klein. Greenberg and Mitchell constantly stress how he tried to maintain the continuity of his thinking with Freud's, although he in fact made many original contributions. Winnicott's much mentioned concepts of the 'transitional object' (for example, a teddy bear), and of the 'illusion' created through it of mother's presence being under the child's control, show traces of Freud's influence. The first, the transitional object, parallels Freud's observation of his grandchild's use of a toy thrown and recovered from the pram, to 'master' the comings and goings of his mother. Freud's view of 'illusion' is rather different from Winnicott's use of it: Freud was emphatic about the need for freedom from illusion, relating it, for example, to religion as a regressive phenomenon (1927c); Winnicott emphasized the freedom that came from being able to create illusion, and the way in which illusion and disillusionment are part of a constant attempt throughout adult life to relate outer and inner reality (see my own book on illusion and belief, Jacobs, 2000).

Fairbairn's clinical practice was classical psychoanalysis, although, as Greenberg and Mitchell put it, he 'felt that most analysts would be rightfully indignant at the suggestion that they minimized concerns about relations with other people in their work with patients. ... His concern was their failure to apply their clinical experience with patients to the most basic of their theoretical principles' (1983: 151).

Fairbairn retained much of Freud's language, even though he was forthright in his rejection of many aspects of Freud's conceptual framework. He adopted the concept of libido, but he changed its aim, so that it became object-seeking rather than pleasure-seeking. Eventually he preferred to see 'the individual in his libidinal capacity (and not libido)' as being object-seeking: 'Pleasure is the signpost to the object but the object is the goal' (Guntrip, 1961: 305). Fairbairn also rejected Freud's construction of the ego from the id, with the later addition of the super-ego. He put forward in its place a unitary ego, which becomes split in the early weeks of life into three parts: that part of the ego that is bound to the object that promises relatedness; that part that is bound to the object as rejecting; and the central ego.

Fairbairn and Winnicott came closer than Klein in their stress on significance of the child's external environment to Freud's early belief in trauma being caused by actual experience. As a consequence they attached less importance than Klein does to Freud's revised position that neurosis is caused less by real traumatic experience and more by the conflicts arising from internalized fantasies, wishes and fears. Freud's emphasis on the place of the father in psychological development appears to have fallen somewhat by the way. Neither Winnicott nor Fairbairn assigned a satisfactory position to the role of the father, except as the supporter of the nursing couple (mother and baby) in Winnicott, or the 'parent without breasts' in Fairbairn (1952: 122). Having corrected Freud's lack of emphasis on the mother, it appears that many of his followers have similarly neglected the second parent, although in more recent years this apparent lack of interest has shown signs of changing (Machtlinger, 1981; and Samuels, from a Jungian perspective, 1985).

Winnicott and Fairbairn, after Klein, are perhaps the most important of the major contributors to object relations theory. They form part of 'the British school', which is to be distinguished from the Kleinian 'English school', both by name and by subscribing not to a set of shared beliefs, but to a shared set of problems. They have much in common, apart from Freud's obvious influence upon their thinking. Each was also Guntrip's analyst, and their therapeutic style is well described by Guntrip (1975). Guntrip's own contribution, apart from his summary of and contribution to the development of object relations (1961), has been the identification of the *retreat* from objects in the schizoid experience (Guntrip, 1968).

His concern for what he saw as the deeply unique experience of being a person, and for the 'spiritual self' (he was formerly a Congregational minister), made Freud's antipathy to religion disturbing to Guntrip. The sociologist Bocock has observed how difficult it has been for many in the churches, who have also made major use of Freud's pioneering work, to follow Freud in what may have been a profoundly accurate analysis of the unconscious motives behind religious beliefs and behaviour (Bocock, 1983: 134). What is interesting is the way in which some thinkers within psychoanalysis have moved beyond the somewhat sterile debate about theology, to interest in the spiritual and the mystical (see, for example, Bion in Symington and Symington, 1996; Eigen, 1998).

Object relations theory now occupies a central position in psychoanalytic thinking, and the precise relationship between these major contributions since Freud and Freud's own theory is not a simple one to disentangle. It is sometimes like looking for the relationship between two artists as far apart in time and style as Rembrandt and Picasso. At first glance they seem to have little connection. But on closer examination there are clear and unmistakable signs of Rembrandt's direct influence in some of Picasso's work. Freud's work remains not just the foundation for current psychoanalytic theory and practice, but also in part maintains its magisterial influence, although, as Greenberg and Mitchell comment, 'psychoanalytic theory is not simply additive; it consists of uniquely fashioned crystallizations of ideas and data, often overlapping but with different centers and organizational principles' (1983: 219–20).

This outline of Freud's influence on and through post-Freudian theory has been limited to psychoanalysis in Britain and the United States. As is the case with other schools or models of therapy, psychoanalysis has spread to many parts of the world, with important contributions that owe much to Freud's pioneering work, in countries as far apart as Japan, Argentina (especially Racker, 1968) and France where Lacan (e.g. 1979) made a distinctive contribution claiming to represent a return to Freud's original concepts and is critical of both ego-psychology and object relations theory; see Roudinesco, 1990).

Group Therapy

Although the development of group therapy cannot be attributed to Freud, he suggested the possibility when he wrote about group psychology (1921c). The title is slightly confusing since *Massenpsychologie* can be translated either as group psychology or mass psychology, and since much of the book is devoted to large organizations such as the army and the church this appears to be where his emphasis lies. Nevertheless, as Schermer argues, 'his reference to various cultural groupings and to the re-evocation of parent–child feelings and sibling rivalry in the transference indicate he was speaking generically of any group, large or small, in which primitive regression takes place' (1994: 13). It was the first time, Schermer writes, that Freud regarded psychoanalysis as both an individual and a group psychology (1994: 14).

Group therapy has developed, like individual therapy, from different theoretical bases, and much psychoanalytic group theory (such as at the Tavistock Institute of Human Relations in London) stems from Bion's understanding of group behaviours (1961), as a defence against psychotic anxiety. It is therefore more Kleinian than Freudian. However, another strand of analytic group therapy is represented by the Institute of Group Analysis, for which the key 'founding' work of Foulkes and Anthony stands 'firmly on the grounds of classical psychoanalysis as founded by Freud' (1957: 17). Foulkes and Anthony distinguish analytic groupwork from non-analytic groupwork by 'the analytic attitude of the therapist (and the guiding principles of his interventions which are developed from psychoanalytic experience), concern with the dynamic unconscious, and the interpretation of resistances, defence reactions, transference, etc.' (1957: 22). They are, however, hesitant to call analytic group psychotherapy 'psychoanalysis', because they see psychoanalysis as 'principally biological and genetic in its approach' and 'the group situation produces powerful and completely new parameters of its own' (1957: 23). The authors produce a useful comparison of the similarities and differences between individual psychoanalysis and group analysis

(1957: 52). Some features are the same (for example, verbal communication, and making the repressed conscious); some features differ only in the numbers involved (for example, multiple transference relationships in groups). Other features are quite different (for example, regression is encouraged by the individual situation, but not by the group situation; the analyst is relatively anonymous in individual work, but more real and interactional in group analysis).

Freud and Feminist Therapy

I have already (pp. 114–19) made clear the strong criticism that has been levelled at Freud's tantalizingly brief and late excursion into women's psychology; at the same time I drew attention to the way in which a number of feminist therapists have developed their own positions from within the psychoanalytic tradition (Eichenbaum and Orbach, 1985; Dinnerstein, 1987; Chodorow, 1978, 1989, 1994, 1996); to these references could be added many others, among whom particular mention should be made of Juliet Mitchell (1974), who draws more upon Freud's drive/conflict theory than, as do the others, upon object relations theory.

Dinnerstein, agrees with Freud that the 'long dependence of the human infant underlies many of the ambiguities, complexities, and internal contradictions of the human situation' (1987: 29). 'The earliest roots of antagonism to women lie in the period before the infant has any clear idea where the self ends and the outside world begins' (1987: 93). Again, like Freud she accepts the closeness of infancy, which is lost as separation from mother occurs and she suggests the need to pay greater attention than he did to the need to mourn the loss of oneness with the mother. Although Dinnerstein is critical of patriarchal society in a way Freud never was, she interprets it partly in terms of the experience of helplessness in infancy: 'In sum, male rule of the world is not a conspiracy imposed by bad, physically strong and mobile, men on good, physically weak and burdened, women … it has been a chronic strain on both sexes …' (1987: 176–7). Men also suffer in this and 'Freud's suffering in it made him take giant steps in a direction that bears closely on the relation between human gender arrangements and human malaise' (1987: 180) – although Freud himself did not see this connection.

In some aspects of her work Dinnerstein extends hints, which are found in Freud's essays, particularly those on feminine psychology. She agrees with Freud on the shift of object-love for a girl from a woman to a man. She believes that a girl's love is more evenly directed to both parents than a boy's, and that a woman's heterosexual jealousy is apt to be more complicated than a man's by homoerotic excitement. She finds some evidence for Freud's suggestion of a girl's 'reproach that her mother did not give her a proper penis – that is to say brought her into the world as a female' (Freud, 1933a: 381). There is, says Dinnerstein, a 'core of truth in the Freudian statement that the girl blames her lack of a penis on the mother' (1987: 52), though she values the penis not mainly as 'a water-toy or in its magic erectile properties ... but rather in the social prerogatives it confers' (1987: 52n). To a girl, father is a 'figure through whom one reaches toward the wider world' (1987: 50), although she also learns she is not welcome in it. Dinnerstein also finds some value in Freud's death instinct, accepting that it is controversial, but finding some dimensions of it a convincing statement of our 'fundamental predicament and related diagnoses of civilization's disease' (1987: 123).

Chodorow too is strongly influenced by certain aspects of Freud's theory: 'Freud's accounts of the psychological destructiveness of bourgeois marriage, gender differentiation and child-rearing practices remain unsurpassed' (1978: 40). She states that 'psychoanalytic theory remains the most coherent, convincing theory of personality development for an understanding of fundamental aspects of the psychology of women in our society, in spite of its biases' (1978: 142). She agrees that daughters have longer and more intense relationships with their mothers than sons have, and 'come to define themselves more in relation to others' (1978: 93). Thus girls are not hindered by this, but enriched in their ability to relate. And although some of the feminist writers have themselves been criticized, again from within psychoanalytic circles (O'Connor and Ryan, 1993) for emphasizing heterosexuality as the norm, Chodorow has herself described the diversity of sexuality, pointing to its recognition by Freud himself, who

> demonstrates for us a range of possible locations within the psychology and social organization of gender and sexuality. In his writing on sexuality and development, his cases, and his social theories, women are young girls, mothers of daughters and mothers of sons, daughters of mothers and daughters of fathers; they are heterosexual, lesbian, sexually inhibited or frigid altogether; they are substitute mothers as nursemaids, servants, or governesses; they are wives, mother-symbols, or whore-like sexual objects of desirous or fearful men. (1994: 3–4)

Psychoanalysis, Sociology and Philosophy

Moving beyond the world of psychotherapy and counselling, it is clear from the constant reference to Freud in the media as well as in a number of different academic disciplines that Freud and his theories have had a major impact upon our present culture. Some of his theories have links with concepts that are the stock-in-trade of other disciplines; for example, Freud's thinking on socialization, or his metapsychology of the structure of the mind, have each had direct relevance for sociology and philosophy respectively. Furthermore, psychoanalysis as a separate discipline, with its own discourse, and with its particular impact upon Western culture and thought, has itself been a rich area of study for philosophers, sociologists and historians (for example, Berger, 1965; Turkle, 1979). At times, of course, it is impossible to disentangle these two areas of interest in psychoanalysis. That a book solely about Freud appears in a series on 'Key Sociologists' (Bocock, 1983), or another in a series of 'Modern Masters' *(sic)* is written by a professor of philosophy (Wollheim, 1971), is an indication of his stature within each discipline, and the attention that he so obviously merits.

In his foreword to Bocock's study of Freud, the series editor has little doubt about the way Freud's ideas about socialization and the family have directed

> much research in this field – sociologists like Talcott Parsons and social-psychologists such as Erikson, taking Freudian theory as the basis of their own work. Similarly, Freud's theories about the relationship between sexuality and culture have proved to be capable of incorporation within radical sociological theories of ideological domination, and sustained extensive debate about gender and sex roles. ... Finally, the clinical concern with psychopathology ... has similarly found direct application in the sociology of mental illness. (Bocock, 1983: 8)

Bocock himself concludes that sociologists such as Parsons, Habermas and Marcuse have nearly always used Freudian theory to 'add and expand upon an already existing theory of society', although some writers are developing what might be called a Freudian social theory retaining 'the emphasis Freud made on the fundamental notion of unconscious wishes, on the need for a concept of rationality and on the social and cultural aspects of psychoanalysis' (Bocock, 1983: 138).

In modern philosophy the debate about Freud's thinking includes those logical positivists who have taken their cue from Wittgenstein and Popper, both like Freud from Vienna, and their 'measured warnings against the heavy reliance of Freudianism upon untestable propositions' (Biddiss, 1977: 262–3); they put psychoanalytic discourse on the same level as the language used in religious and moral thinking. Others are more enthusiastic about psychoanalysis – John Wisdom, for example, a philosopher of science and the author of a considerable number of publications about aspects of the philosophy of psychoanalysis (for example, Wisdom, 1963). In its turn psychoanalysis has been applied to understanding philosophers, examining, to take just one example, the unconscious source of Kant's philosophy (Feuer, 1970: 76–125).

The application of Freud's psychoanalytic work to other disciplines can also be seen in the work of the theologian Paul Tillich (1957), and in the twin pursuits of psycho-biography (Runyan, 1982) and psycho-history (Albin, 1980), both taking their lead from the extended Freudian psycho-social approach in Erik Erikson (1950). The list of thinkers who are in one way or another involved in integrating Freud's thinking with their own special area of study is a long one, and in the end might even cease to have meaning given the pervasive influence of Freud on twentieth-century culture. Nevertheless, mention might be made of Jean Piaget and his psychology of cognitive development; Chomsky, Lacan and the study of linguistics; Lévi-Strauss, Margaret Mead and anthropology. Little wonder that the historian of ideas, Michael Biddiss, can describe Freud's work as 'one of the greatest intellectual revolutions of the early twentieth century' (1977: 56).

It is important to bear in mind, however, that if Freud is often an influence in his own right, there are other instances where his own search was part of a general intellectual trend, so that in his exploration Freud ran parallel with the questioning that was taking place in other disciplines: many of these disciplines appear to converge, arriving at similar conclusions, but none are able to claim priority. For example, Freud's demonstration of the irrationality of the human mind, often dictated by unconscious processes with their own rules of illogicality, was a challenge to certainty and scientific optimism, even if at the same time Freud looked for patterns to the unconscious. In a simultaneous but independent movement, scientific laws, also acknowledged as constructs of frail reason, were challenged, especially in the realm of physics; and new patterns such as relativity were developed. Similar movements within philosophy, politics (anarchism), sociology, art (such as surrealism, perhaps seen at its most 'Freudian' in Salvador Dali), literature (for example, Proust and Joyce) and music (for example, Schoenberg) are all capable of 'intimating that many significant aspects of reality might correspond more closely to the dream world as charted by Freud than to experience as more conventionally conceived' (Biddiss, 1977: 177). Biddiss also highlights the way that 'elucidation of the ultimate inseparability of thought, emotion and action has been one of the most impressive intellectual endeavours of this epoch, carried on even in fields beyond that of its most explicit and dramatic study by Freud and the post-Freudians' (1977: 19).

Psychoanalysis, Literature and the Arts

An impish streak almost tempted me to include among Freud's works the case history which appears in D.M. Thomas' novel *The White Hotel*. It is in fact entirely fictional, although it is masterly in its expression of Freud's writing and thinking, just as the author of *The White Hotel* praises Freud's case histories as being 'masterly works of literature, apart from anything else' (Thomas, 1981: 6). This interplay between fact and fiction is to be expected in two disciplines that are centred upon human character, human relationships and communication through the word. Freud's attempts to map the features and structures of personality, and to chart the emotional impact of life events, have their parallels in the psychological awareness of the nineteenth-century novel. Fromm sees Freud as 'the first to analyse character scientifically rather than artistically as his novelist-predecessors had done' (1980: 55).

Freud was himself interested in the psychology of the creative artist. He observed that the novelist works upon inner themes, and expresses them through the medium of writing, more constructively but similarly to the neurotic's expression of inner personal dramas (1908e). Novels are more or less disguised expressions of personal relationships, of internal and external conflicts, sometimes present within the author, sometimes present within those of the author's acquaintance. 'The psychological novel in general no doubt owes its special nature to the inclination of the modern writer to split up his ego, by self-observation, into many part-egos, and, in consequence, to personify the conflicting currents of his mental life in several heroes' (Freud, 1908e: 138). The line between fact and fiction is a thin one, once one gets beneath the veneer of the art of conscious and unconscious disguise. Thomas' case history in *The White Hotel* may be fictional in that Freud did not write it; but, if Freud was right, it is also not pure fiction: it is in part the product of Thomas' own experience.

It is not surprising that the work of understanding the artist's creation also becomes one of interpretation of the artist. Gay neatly summarizes Freud's research into literature as touching upon 'the three principal dimensions of aesthetic experience: the psychology of the protagonists, the psychology of the audience, and the psychology of the maker. These dimensions necessarily implicate and illuminate one another' (1989: 318). There is a close link between the enterprise of the literary critic and that of the analyst, as well as, Wright observes, between that of the patient and the reader: 'Both ... are engaged in pursuing undecidable meanings: ambiguity, ambivalence, fantasy, illusion and play [later she adds jokes to this list] are their joint stock-in-trade' (1984: 175).

It is obvious, from the reading of many twentieth-century novels, how much Freudian ways of understanding have entered the consciousness both of the characters and of their authors. There is no need to illustrate the extent of this, although the following words, spoken by a lecturer in English literature in the novel *Possession*, both typify and summarize that influence:

> In every age, there must be truths people can't fight – whether or not they want to, whether or not they will go on being truths in the future. We live in the truth of what Freud discovered. Whether we like it or not. However we've modified it. We aren't really free to suppose – to imagine – he could possibly have been wrong about human nature. In particulars, surely – but not in the large plan. (Byatt, 1990: 254)

Byatt is a novelist as well as a literary critic. Just as the novelist has been influenced by psychoanalytic theory, so too has the critic been considerably influenced by psychoanalytic method. Felman (1982) has argued that literature and psychoanalysis are linked, in the sense that each constitutes the other's 'unconscious'. Some analysts and critics have applied the psychoanalytic method of interpretation directly to authors, artists and their creations. Freud's study of *The Gradiva* (1907a), Leonardo da Vinci (1910c) or Michelangelo's 'Moses' (1914b), Bonaparte's study of Edgar Allan Poe (1949), or D.H. Lawrence's study of American literature (1977) employ what Wright calls an 'id-psychology' approach to the artistic, seeing it as the return of the repressed, the expression of infantile wishes (1984: 37). Others employ an ego-psychological approach (Kris, 1952), showing that 'artistic activity derives from a controlled play with infantile material' (Wright, 1984: 56).

Of even greater influence now in literary criticism than the traditional psychoanalytic approaches to literature, is the psychoanalytic structural approach, strongly influenced by the work of the French psychoanalyst Lacan, applied much more to the text and the interplay between the text and the reader, 'without either one mastering the other, as was the case with classical applied psychoanalysis' (Wright, 1984: 131). In Lacan, felt by many French psychoanalysts to be the greatest psychoanalytic thinker since Freud, there is a deep commitment to Freud, particularly to the series of oppositions which Freud uncovered between 'normal/pathological, sanity/insanity, real/imaginary, experience/dream, conscious/unconscious, life/death. ... Freud's investigations deconstruct these oppositions ... Understanding of the marginal deviant term becomes a condition of understanding the supposed prior term' (Culler, quoted in Wright, 1984: 138). Similar use has been made of what is technically known as structuralist and poststructuralist psychoanalytic criticism in connection with art (particularly the work of the surrealists) and film (e.g. Kaplan, 1990). These are all specialist applications of psychoanalysis which require their own explication, and which it is obviously impossible to summarize adequately here. In some cases (for example, the work of Lacan, 1979), there can be difficulty in understanding the conceptual frameworks and the language that these highly innovative thinkers use (but see Turkle, 1979), although this does not in itself alter the huge significance that Freudian ideas have had in the analysis of the arts.

Key Features in Freud's Influence

In addition to the obvious influence of Freud's theories upon the development of psychoanalysis and psychotherapy, and upon other forms of intellectual pursuit, his ideas and techniques have entered the more generic field of therapy, even where it is practised within schools and according to methods which are avowedly not psychoanalytic. Those who call themselves psychodynamic make the most obvious use of Freudian, Kleinian, and object relations theories, although they may also prefer to align themselves with Jungian theories too. Some of those styled psychodynamic adhere strongly to the psychoanalytic model, while others, such as the present author, prefer to use the psychoanalytic as a base from which to move critically towards an integrative position. Therefore each therapist or counsellor will make their own use, some extensively and some minimally, of Freud's principles and concepts, in some cases perhaps without recognizing their source. Terms such as projection, splitting, repression, displacement, denial; or aspects of the structure of personality such as 'parts' or even the somewhat dated id, ego and super-ego; or descriptive terms such as the obsessional character, the hysteric, dependency, voyeurism, exhibitionism, fetishism; or even once strictly psychoanalytic terms such as 'transference' and 'counter-transference' – all these and more appear with regularity in conversations between therapists, in supervision, and even in the language some clients use, well beyond Freudian circles.

Stepping aside from a hitherto more objective stance, what might I choose to stress as valuable from the vast treasury of

Freudian theory and practice? In the therapeutic session itself we might choose the use of free association, not in the sense of mindless psycho-babble, but in the encouragement to the client to be more spontaneous, and to the therapist to listen with that free-floating attention which Freud saw as the counterpart to free association. We might also select, especially since it is also singled out now as probably the most significant factor in the effectiveness of therapy, the centrality of the therapeutic relationship, including those elements that appear to reflect not only the client's past, but also the therapist's, and to reflect as well external and internalized relationships in client and therapist, through the phenomenon of transference and counter-transference (Racker, 1968): 'it was Freud's genius to observe this phenomenon' (Fromm, 1980: 39). We might also want to extend that insight to the phenomenon of transference in everyday life.

In understanding the client, we might choose to stress Freud's recognition of the conflict between parts of the personality; or the weight he attached to the different impulses that find expression in relationships, particularly Eros and Thanatos, sexuality and aggression, love and death, whether expressed in the actual, in displacement and sublimation, all as much part of being human for us as it was for Freud. We might find it difficult to avoid the importance attached to childhood experience, which in its turn may have given us a heightened awareness of the feelings and needs of children, and of the child in the adult; similarly, the more general influence of the past upon the present would be a difficult aspect to neglect. The significance of the symbolic and the perpetual surfacing of the triangular nature of relationships, whether external or internal, part-object or whole person, the value of story, and the richness of language might also figure high on the list.

For understanding ourselves as therapists and counsellors, we could do no better than to follow Freud in underlining the necessity for self-awareness, and to emulate the self-analysis that he was continually engaged upon, with the aid of trusted colleagues; we would be foolish to forget the importance of the unconscious, and what Fromm highlights as 'the discrepancy between thinking and being. ... Freud's discovery was that what we think is not necessarily identical with what we are' (1980: 23); we might even, paradoxically, see the truth in Freud's mistrust of the rational: 'most of us live in a world of self-deception in which we take our thoughts as representing reality' (Fromm, 1980: 23). The combination of trying to remain objective, and yet opening up to the intuitive and the possibility of a different type of knowledge, deceptively called insight, is a vital aspect of Freud's model that therapists will want to emulate.

Each therapist will have his or her own set of choices from Freud's treasury. What is undeniable is that, as in Auden's memorial poem for Freud, he and his work have created 'a whole climate of opinion', with which in its particulars we remain free to agree or disagree.

The Wider World

Some of Freud's thinking and certain psychoanalytic concepts reach a far wider audience than any academic discipline or any system of psychotherapy – through those who have created greater and lesser works of art and of literature, and through theatre, film and television (even through advertising). What Freud started to uncover, even if not studied through Freud's own words, has stretched (and on the way sometimes been distorted) into popular culture and consciousness, and, if I can use such a phrase without appearing to attribute it to Freud, into the popular unconscious. There is even a popular version of psychoanalysis, which emulates analysts in 'interpreting' behaviour.

No other person from the field of therapy and counselling has achieved this degree of exposure. This means, as I began by stating at the outset, that it is impossible for any counsellor or therapist, of whatever persuasion, to ignore Freud's influence, even if it has only been understood in popular form, since it is being brought daily to sessions as part of the cultural background of nearly every client. Even if the Oedipus complex were only a figment of Freud's imagination, it has become part of the consciousness of many people. Where Freud appears to have understood the human psyche correctly, this may help to explain why some of his ideas seem to 'fit'; but even if he has got it wrong, his ideas have triggered off a trace of recognition, and perhaps provided, if nothing else, support for the attempt to understand ourselves. Because what Freud said, or is thought to have said, has such a popular appeal, the version which people sometimes express itself tells the therapist or counsellor something about the meaning which their clients attach to their inner experiences and the impact upon them of external events.

Tempting though it is, given the way in which, like a Colossus, he bestrides the twentieth century, to idealize the man, to eulogize his work and to universalize his influence, it is refreshing to recall Freud's own more modest assessment of himself in the final paragraph of his autobiography: 'Looking back, then, over the patchwork of my life's labours, I can say that I have made many beginnings and thrown out many suggestions. Something will come of them in the future, though I cannot myself tell whether it will be much or little.' The last sentence, one which he added to the 1935 edition, reads: 'I can, however, express a hope that I have opened up a pathway for an important advance in our knowledge' (1925d: 255).

Appendix: Reading Freud

One of Freud's major problems (or would be if he were alive to witness it) is that many of those who quote him have failed to read anything he wrote. Instead they speak from passing knowledge, from reviews and critiques of his work, and from the popular view of him that pervades our culture. But Freud cries out to be read, for a variety of reasons. Firstly his literary style, in most of his work, is brilliant. Freud is witty, argues with himself, and employs a turn of phrase, which is sometimes tongue in cheek, sometimes profoundly moving, and sometimes touches the deeper mysteries of our thinking. This way with words is even more evident in the new translation of some of his major texts in the new edition of Freud published by Penguin Classics, under the general editorship of Adam Phillips. The translator of one of the books writes: 'The experience of translating *The Psychopathology of Everyday Life* has left me with a great admiration for the man, a closer knowledge of his time, and a sense of finding him far more approachable than I did before' (1901b/2002: xliii). 'To read him is to be spellbound', writes Grayling in an otherwise deeply critical article on Freud's ideas (2002: 7), triggered by the new Penguin translation. The added advantage of the new Penguin Classics is that the introduction to each of Freud's texts is more critically aware than those by the editors of the Standard Edition.

Given that Freud wrote so much, where might the new reader start? In the old translation, Peter Gay's *The Freud Reader* (1995) complements his magisterial biography (Gay, 1989). Here the reader can sample extracts from Freud's work. Alternatively, or perhaps with the appetite whetted, the next step is to choose between either

Freud's lectures, delivered in the first case, and written in the second set, for the lay audience:

Freud, S. (1916–17) *Introductory Lectures on Psychoanalysis*. Penguin Freud Library, Volume 1.
Freud, S. (1933a) *New Introductory Lectures on Psychoanalysis*. Penguin Freud Library, Volume 2.

or the early American lectures:

Freud, S. (1910a/2001) *Five Lectures on Psychoanalysis*. Standard Edition, Volume XI, London: Virago; also found in *Two Short Accounts of Psychoanalysis* (1962), London: Penguin.

Or to choose his case-studies, which, as I have noted in Chapter 2, Freud himself thought read like novellas: here the obvious books to read are the early studies from the formative period with Breuer, and his later studies, controversial though some of them have become:

Freud, S. and Breuer, J. (1895d) *Studies on Hysteria*. Penguin Freud Library, Volume 3.

Freud, S. (1905e) 'Dora' and (1909b) 'Little Hans', Penguin Freud Library, Volume 8.

Freud, S. (1909d) 'The Ratman'; (1911c, 1912a) Schreber; (1918b) 'The Wolf Man'; and *The Psychogenesis of a Case of Homosexuality in a Woman* (1920a) Penguin Freud Library, Volume 9.

The new translations in Penguin Classics feature the Schreber case (Freud, 1911c/2002, in fact Freud's analysis of written memoirs of a psychotic breakdown) and *The 'Wolfman' and Other Cases* (Freud, 2002), which includes 'The Ratman' and 'Little Hans'.

Freud's papers on technique have hitherto been available only in the Standard Edition, although with the publication of the Standard Edition by Virago in 2001, this vast corpus has been made much more accessible. The papers on technique are also published by Penguin Classics in the volume rather inappropriately named *Wild Analysis* (Freud, 2002) and are used in that translation wherever possible in this book. The following papers, found in that book or the Standard Edition, Volumes XII and XXIII, throw considerable light upon Freud's ideas on the practice of therapy:

Freud, S. (1911e/2002) 'On the uses of dream interpretation in psychoanalysis', in *Wild Analysis* (2002). London: Penguin Classics.

Freud, S. (1912b/2002) 'On the dynamics of transference', in *Wild Analysis* (2002). London: Penguin Classics.

Freud, S. (1912e/2002) 'Advice to doctors on psychoanalytic treatment', in *Wild Analysis* (2002). London: Penguin Classics.

Freud, S. (1913c/2002) 'On initiating treatment', in *Wild Analysis* (2002). London: Penguin Classics.

Freud, S. (1914g/2001) *Remembering, Repeating and Working Through*. Standard Edition, Volume XII. London: Virago.

Freud, S. (1937c/2002) 'Analysis terminable and interminable', in *Wild Analysis* (2002). London: Penguin Classics.

Freud, S. (1937d/2002) 'Constructions in analysis', in *Wild Analysis* (2002). London: Penguin Classics.

Freud's early work still provides much by way of illustration and explanation:

Freud, S. (1900a) *The Interpretation of Dreams*. Penguin Freud Library, Volume 4.

Freud, S. (1901b/2002) *The Psychopathology of Everyday Life*. London: Penguin Classics.
Freud, S. (1905d) *Three Essays on the Theory of Sexuality*. Penguin Freud Library, Volume 7.

Much of Freud's most relevant writing is adapted for slightly more 'popular' presentation in the *Introductory Lectures* or the *New Introductory Lectures*, but can be read in its fuller form by those wishing to follow up particular topics. Some of these and those referred to above are also due to be published by Penguin Classics in new translations:

Gender and Feminism

Freud, S. (1925j) *Some Psychical Consequences of the Anatomical Distinction between the Sexes*. Penguin Freud Library, Volume 7.
Freud, S. (1931b) *Female Sexuality*. Penguin Freud Library, Volume 7.

Religion

Freud, S. (1907b) *Obsessive Actions and Religious Practices*. Penguin Freud Library, Volume 13.
Freud, S. (1927c) *The Future of an Illusion*. Penguin Freud Library, Volume 12.

Personality Structure

Freud, S. (1923b) *The Ego and the Id*. Penguin Freud Library, Volume 11.

The Individual and Society

Freud, S. (1930a/2002) *Civilization and Its Discontents*. London: Penguin Classics.

Freud's correspondence with a number of important figures, such as Jung, Jones, Ferenczi, and others is available through various publications. If I have to single out one book of letters, perhaps the most appropriate is the one that collects together the thinking which in a sense started it all:

Masson, J. (ed.) (1985) *The Complete Letters of Sigmund Freud to Wilhelm Fliess*. Cambridge, Mass.: Belknap Press.

References

Albin, M. (ed.) (1980) *New Directions in Psychohistory*. Lexington, Mass.: Lexington Books.

Alexander, F. and French, T.M. (1946) *Psychoanalytic Therapy: Principles and Application*. New York: Ronald Press.

Badcock, C.R. (1980) *The Psychoanalysis of Culture*. Oxford: Blackwell.

Barron, J.W., Beaumont, R., Goldsmith, G.N., Good, M.I., Pyles, R.L., Rizzuto, A.-M. and Smith, H.F. (1991) 'Sigmund Freud: The Secrets of Nature and the Nature of Secrets', *International Review of Psycho-Analysis*, 18: 143–63.

Berger, P. (1965) 'Towards a sociological understanding of psychoanalysis', *Social Research*, 32: 26–41.

Bettelheim, B. (1983) *Freud and Man's Soul*. London: Chatto and Windus.

Biddiss, M.D. (1977) *The Age of the Masses*. London: Penguin Books.

Bion, W.R. (1961) *Experiences in Groups and Other Papers*. London: Tavistock Publications.

Blanck, G. and Blanck, R. (1994) *Ego Psychology: Theory and Practice* (second edition). New York: Columbia University Press.

Blum, H.P. (1992) 'Report on the Sigmund Freud archives', *Bulletin of the International Psychoanalytic Association*, 73: 410–11.

Bocock, R. (1983) *Sigmund Freud*. London: Tavistock Publications/Horwood.

Bonaparte, M. (1949) *The Life and Works of Edgar Allan Poe*. London: Imago.

Bonaparte, M., Freud, A. and Kris, E. (eds) (1954) *The Origins of Psychoanalysis: Letters to Wilhelm Fliess, Drafts and Notes 1877–1902*. London: Imago.

Brennen, C. (1993) 'Dreams in clinical psychoanalytic practice', in S. Flanders (ed.), *The Dream Discourse Today*. London: Routledge.

Brook, A. (1995) 'Explanation in the hermeneutic science', *International Journal of Psycho-Analysis*, 76: 519–32.

Byatt, A.S. (1990) *Possession*. London: Chatto and Windus.

Carvalho, R. (1982) 'Paternal deprivation in relation to narcissistic damage', *Journal of Analytical Psychology*, 27.

Casement, A. (2001) *Carl Gustav Jung*. London: Sage Publications.

Cheshire, N. and Thomä, H. (1991) 'Metaphor, neologism and "Open Texture": implications for translating Freud's scientific thought', *International Review of Psycho-Analysis*, 18: 429–55.

Chodorow, N. (1978) *The Reproduction of Mothering*. London: Yale University Press.

Chodorow, N. (1989) *Feminism and Psychoanalytic Theory*. New Haven, CT: Yale University Press.

Chodorow, N. (1994) *Femininities, Masculinities, Sexualities*. London: Free Association Books.

Chodorow, N. (1996) 'Theoretical gender and clinical gender: epistemological reflections on the psychology of women', *Journal of the American Psychoanalytic Association*, 44S: 215–38.

Clark, R. (1980) *Freud: The Man and the Cause*. London: Cape/Weidenfeld and Nicolson.

Clarkson, P. and Mackewn, J. (1993) *Fritz Perls*. London: Sage Publications.

Coren, A. (2001) *Short-Term Psychotherapy: a Psychodynamic Approach*. London: Palgrave.

Crews, F. (1995) *The Memory Wars: Freud's Legacy in Dispute*. New York: New York Review of Books.

Deutsch, H. (1940) 'Freud and his pupils – a footnote to the history of the psychoanalytic movement'. *Psychoanalytic Quarterly*, 9: 184–94.

Deutsch, H. (1973) *Confrontations with Myself*. New York: W.W. Norton.

Dinnage, R. (1989) *One to One*. London: Penguin Books.

Dinnerstein, D. (1987) *The Rocking of the Cradle and the Ruling of the World*. London: The Women's Press.

Dupont, J. (ed.) (1995) *The Clinical Diary of Sandor Ferenczi*. Cambridge, Mass.: Harvard University Press.

Efron, A. (1977) 'Freud's self-analysis and the nature of psychoanalytic criticism', *International Review of Psycho-Analysis*, 4: 253–80.

Eichenbaum, L. and Orbach, S. (1985) *Understanding Women*. London: Penguin Books.

Eigen, M. (1998) *The Psychoanalytic Mystic*. London: Free Association Books.

Emde, R.N. and Fonagy, P. (1997) 'An emerging culture for psychoanalytic research?' *International Journal of Psycho-Analysis*, 78: 643–51.

Erikson, E. (1950) *Childhood and Society*. New York: Norton.

Eysenck, H.J. (1952) 'The effects of psychotherapy: an evaluation', *Journal of Consulting Psychology*, 40: 317.

Eysenck, H.J. (1953) *Uses and Abuses of Psychology*. London: Penguin Books.

Eysenck, H.J. (1963) 'Psychoanalysis – myth or science?', in S. Rachman (ed.), *Critical Essays on Psychoanalysis*. Oxford: Pergamon.

Eysenck, H.J. (1965) 'The effects of psychotherapy', *International Journal of Psychiatry*, 1: 99–142.

Fairbairn, W.R.D. (1952) *Psychoanalytic Studies of the Personality*. London: Tavistock Publications.

Felman, S. (1982) 'To open the question', in S. Felman (ed.), *Literature and Psychoanalysis: The Question of Reading, Otherwise*. Baltimore, MD: The John Hopkins Press.

Feuer, L. (1970) 'Lawless sensations and categorical defenses: the unconscious sources of Kant's philosophy', in C. Hanly and M. Lazerowitz (eds), *Psychoanalysis and Philosophy*. New York: International Universities Press.

Flanders, S. (ed.) (1993) *The Dream Discourse Today*. London: Routledge.

Foulkes, S. and Anthony, E. (1957) *Group Psychotherapy: The Psychoanalytic Approach*. London: Penguin Books.

Freud, A. (1936) *The Ego and the Mechanisms of Defence*. London: Hogarth Press.

Freud, E. (ed.) (1961) *Letters of Sigmund Freud (1873–1939)*. London: Hogarth Press.

Freud, S. (1900a) *The Interpretation of Dreams*. Penguin Freud Library, Volume 4.

Freud, S. (1901b/2002) *The Psychopathology of Everyday Life*. London: Penguin Classics.

Freud, S. (1905d) *Three Essays on the Theory of Sexuality*. Penguin Freud Library, Volume 7.

Freud, S. (1905e) *Fragment of an Analysis of a Case of Hysteria*. Penguin Freud Library, Volume 8.

Freud, S. (1907a) *Delusions and Dreams in Jensen's 'Gradiva'*. Penguin Freud Library, Volume 14.

Freud, S. (1907b) *Obsessive Actions and Religious Practices*. Penguin Freud Library, Volume 13.

Freud, S. (1908d/2002) '"Civilized" sexual morality and modern nervous illness', in *Civilization and its Discontents* (2002). London: Penguin Classics.

Freud, S. (1908e) *Writers and Daydreaming*. Penguin Freud Library, Volume 14.

Freud, S. (1909b/2002) 'Analysis of a phobia in a five-year-old boy ("Little Hans")', in *The 'Wolfman' and Other Cases* (2002) London: Penguin Classics.

Freud, S. (1909d/2002) 'Some remarks on a case of obsessive-compulsive neurosis (The "Ratman")', in *The 'Wolfman' and Other Cases* (2002). London: Penguin Classics.

Freud, S. (1910a/2001) *Five Lectures on Psychoanalysis*. Standard Edition, Volume XI, London: Virago; and in *Two Short Accounts of Psychoanalysis* (1962). London: Penguin.

Freud, S. (1910c) *Leonardo da Vinci and a Memory of His Childhood*. Penguin Freud Library, Volume 14.

Freud, S. (1910h) *A Special Type of Choice of Object Made by Men*. Penguin Freud Library, Volume 7.

Freud, S. (1910k/2002) 'On "Wild" psychoanalysis', in *Wild Analysis* (2002). London: Penguin Classics.

Freud, S. (1911b) *Formulations on the Two Principles of Mental Functioning*. Penguin Freud Library, Volume 11.

Freud, S. (1911c/2002) *The Schreber Case*. London: Penguin Classics.

Freud, S. (1911e/2002) 'On the uses of dream interpretation in psychoanalysis', in *Wild Analysis* (2002). London: Penguin Classics.

Freud, S. (1912a/2002) 'Postscript', in *The Schreber Case* (2002). London: Penguin Classics.

Freud, S. (1912b/2002) 'On the dynamics of transference', in *Wild Analysis* (2002). London: Penguin Classics.

Freud, S. (1912e/2002) 'Advice to doctors on psychoanalytic treatment', in *Wild Analysis* (2002). London: Penguin Classics.

Freud, S. (1912f/2001) *Contributions to a Discussion on Masturbation*. Standard Edition, Volume XII, London: Virago.

Freud, S. (1912–13) *Totem and Taboo*. Penguin Freud Library, Volume 13.

Freud, S. (1913c/2002) 'On initiating treatment', in *Wild Analysis*. London: Penguin Classics.

Freud, S. (1914b) *The Moses of Michelangelo*. Penguin Freud Library, Volume 14.

Freud, S. (1914d) *On the History of the Psychoanalytic Movement*. Penguin Freud Library, Volume 15.

Freud, S. (1914g/2001) *Remembering, Repeating and Working Through*. Standard Edition, Volume XII, London: Virago.

Freud, S. (1915a/2002) 'Observations on love transference', in *Wild Analysis* (2002). London: Penguin Classics.

Freud, S. (1915b) *Thoughts for the Times on War and Death*. Penguin Freud Library, Volume 12.

Freud, S. (1915d) *Repression*. Penguin Freud Library, Volume 11.

Freud, S. (1915e) *The Unconscious*. Penguin Freud Library, Volume 11.

Freud, S. (1916–17) *Introductory Lectures on Psychoanalysis*. Penguin Freud Library, Volume 1.

Freud, S. (1917e) *Mourning and Melancholia*. Penguin Freud Library, Volume 11.

Freud, S. (1918b/2002) 'From the history of an infantile neurosis (The "Wolfman")', in *The 'Wolfman' and Other Cases* (2002). Penguin Freud Library, Volume 9.

Freud, S. (1920a) *The Psychogenesis of a Case of Homosexuality in a Woman.* Penguin Freud Library, Volume 9.

Freud, S. (1920g) *Beyond the Pleasure Principle.* Penguin Freud Library, Volume 11.

Freud, S. (1921c) *Group Psychology and the Analysis of the Ego.* Penguin Freud Library, Volume 12.

Freud, S. (1923a) *Two Encyclopedia Articles.* Penguin Freud Library, Volume 15.

Freud, S. (1923b) *The Ego and the Id.* Penguin Freud Library, Volume 11.

Freud, S. (1923e) *The Infantile Genital Organization.* Penguin Freud Library, Volume 7.

Freud, S. (1924d) *The Dissolution of the Oedipus Complex.* Penguin Freud Library, Volume 7.

Freud, S. (1924f) *A Short Account of Psychoanalysis.* Penguin Freud Library, Volume 15.

Freud, S. (1925d) *An Autobiographical Study.* Penguin Freud Library, Volume 15.

Freud, S. (1925e/2002) 'Resistance to psychoanalysis', in *Wild Analysis* (2002). London: Penguin Classics.

Freud, S. (1925j) *Some Psychical Consequences of the Anatomical Distinction between the Sexes.* Penguin Freud Library, Volume 7.

Freud, S. (1926e/2002) 'The question of lay analysis', in *Wild Analysis.* London: Penguin Classics.

Freud, S. (1927a/2002) 'Postscript to "The question of lay analysis"', in *Wild Analysis* (2002). London: Penguin Classics.

Freud, S. (1927c) *The Future of an Illusion.* Penguin Freud Library, Volume 12.

Freud, S. (1927e) *Fetishism.* Penguin Freud Library, Volume 7.

Freud, S. (1930a/2002) *Civilization and Its Discontents.* London: Penguin Classics.

Freud, S. (1931b) *Female Sexuality.* Penguin Freud Library, Volume 7.

Freud, S. (1933a) *New Introductory Lectures on Psychoanalysis.* Penguin Freud Library, Volume 2.

Freud, S. (1933b) *Why War?* Penguin Freud Library, Volume 12.

Freud, S. (1937c/2001) *Analysis Terminable and Interminable.* Standard Edition, Volume XXIII. London: Virago.

Freud, S. (1937c/2002) 'Analysis terminable and interminable', in *Wild Analysis* (2002). London: Penguin Classics.

Freud, S. (1937d/2002) 'Constructions in analysis', in *Wild Analysis* (2002). London: Penguin Classics.

Freud, S. (1939a) *Moses and Monotheism.* Penguin Freud Library, Volume 13.

Freud, S. (1940a) *An Outline of Psychoanalysis.* Penguin Freud Library, Volume 15.

Freud, S. and Breuer, J. (1895d) *Studies on Hysteria.* Penguin Freud Library, Volume 3.

Friedman, L.J. (1999) *Identity's Architect: a Biography of Erik H. Erikson.* London: Free Association Books.

Fromm, E. (1966) *The Art of Loving.* London: Unwin Books.

Fromm, E. (1980) *Greatness and Limitations of Freud's Thought.* London: Jonathan Cape.

Gay, P. (1987) *A Godless Jew.* London: Yale University Press.

Gay, P. (1989) *Freud: A Life for Our Time.* London: Macmillan.

Gay, P. (ed.) (1995) *The Freud Reader.* London: Vintage.

Gill, M. (1991) 'Merton Gill speaks his mind', *The American Psychoanalyst*, 25(1): 17–21.

Gilligan, C. (1982) *In a Different Voice.* Cambridge, Mass.: Harvard University Press.

Goetz, B. (1975) 'That is all I have to say about Freud: Bruno Goetz's reminiscences of Sigmund Freud', *International Review of Psycho-Analysis*, 2: 139–43.

Graf, M. (1942) 'Reminiscences of Professor Sigmund Freud', *Psychoanalytic Quarterly*, 9, 465–76.

Grayling, A.C. (2002) 'Scientist or storyteller?' *Guardian Review*, 22 June 2002, 5–7.

Greenberg, J.R. and Mitchell, S.A. (1983) *Object Relations in Psychoanalytic Theory*. Cambridge, Mass.: Harvard University Press.

Guntrip, H. (1961) *Personality Structure and Human Interaction*. London: Hogarth Press.

Guntrip, H. (1968) *Schizoid Phenomena, Object Relations and the Self*. London: Hogarth Press.

Guntrip, H. (1971) *Psychoanalytic Theory, Therapy and the Self*. New York: Basic Books.

Guntrip, H. (1975) 'My experience of analysis with Fairbairn and Winnicott', *International Review of Psycho-Analysis*, 2: 145–56.

Hartmann, H. (1939) *Ego Psychology and the Problem of Adaptation*. New York: International Universities Press.

Hollitscher, W. (1939) 'The concept of rationalization – (some remarks on the analytical criticism of thought)', *International Journal of Psycho-Analysis*, 20: 330–2.

Jacobs, M. (1995) *D.W. Winnicott*. London: Sage Publications.

Jacobs, M. (2000) *Illusion: a Psychodynamic Interpretation of Thinking and Belief*. London: Whurr.

Jacobson, E. (1964) *The Self and the Object World*. London: Hogarth Press.

Jones, E. (1964) *The Life and Work of Sigmund Freud*. London: Penguin Books (abridged edition of three volumes published by Hogarth Press).

Josephs, L. (1989) 'The world of the concrete – a comparative approach', *Contemporary Psychoanalysis*, 25: 477–500.

Jung, C.G. (1967) *Memories, Dreams and Reflections*. London: Collins (Fontana).

Kaplan, E.A. (ed.) (1990) *Psychoanalysis and Cinema*. London: Routledge.

Kardiner, A. (1958) 'Freud - the man I knew, the scientist, and his influence', in B. Nelson (ed.), *Freud and the Twentieth Century*. London: Allen and Unwin.

Kazin, A. (1958) 'The Freudian revolution', in B. Nelson (ed.), *Freud and the Twentieth Century*. London: Allen and Unwin.

Kernberg, O. (1976) *Object Relations Theory and Clinical Psychoanalysis*. New York: Jason Aronson.

Kernberg, O. (1980) *Internal World and External Reality*. New York: Jason Aronson.

Kernberg, O. (1986) 'Institutional problems of psychoanalytic education', *Journal of the American Psychoanalytic Association*, 34: 799–834.

Kernberg, O. (1996) 'Thirty methods to destroy the creativity of psychoanalytic candidates', *International Journal of Psycho-Analysis*, 77: 1031–40.

King, P. and Steiner, R. (eds) (1991) *The Freud–Klein Controversies 1941–45*. London: Routledge.

Klein, M. (1932) *The Psychoanalysis of Children*. London: Hogarth Press.

Kline, P. (1981) *Fact and Fantasy in Freudian Theory* (second edition). London: Methuen.

Kohon, G. (ed.) (1986) *The British School of Psycho-Analysis. The Independent Tradition*. London: Free Association Books.

Kohut, H. (1971) *The Analysis of the Self*. New York: International Universities Press.

Kris, E. (1952) *Psychoanalytic Explorations in Art*. New York: International Universities Press.

Lacan, J. (1979) *The Four Fundamental Concepts of Psychoanalysis*. London: Penguin Books.

Lampl-de-Groot, J. (1976) 'Personal experiences with psychoanalytical technique and theory during the last half century', *Psychoanalytic Study of the Child*, 31: 283–96.

Lawrence, D.H. (1977) *Studies in Classical American Literature*. London: Penguin Books.

Lear, J. (1996) 'The memory wars: Freud's legacy in dispute (Review)', *Journal of American Psychoanalytic Association*. 44: 580–7.

Lehmann, H. (1983) 'Reflections on Freud's reaction to the death of his mother', *Psychoanalytic Quarterly*, 52: 237–49.

Lomas, P. (1973) *True and False Experience*. London: Allen Lane.

Lomas, P. (1987) *The Limits of Interpretation*. London: Penguin Books.

McGuire, W. (ed.) (1974) *The Freud/Jung Letters: The Correspondence between Sigmund Freud and C.G. Jung. London:* Hogarth Press/Routledge and Kegan Paul.

Machtlinger, V.J. (1981) 'The father in psychoanalytic theory', in M.E. Lamb (ed.), *The Role of the Father in Child Development* (second edition, revised). New York: John Wiley.

Malan, D.H. (1963) A *Study of Brief Psychotherapy*. London: Tavistock Publications.

Malan, D.H. and Osimo, F. (1992) *Psychodynamics, Training and Outcome in Brief Psychotherapy*. Oxford: Butterworth/Heinemann.

Masson, J. (1984) *The Assault on Truth: Freud's Suppression of the Seduction Theory*. London: Faber.

Masson, J. (ed.) (1985) *The Complete Letters of Sigmund Freud to Wilhelm Fliess*. Cambridge, Mass.: Belknap Press.

Michels, R. (1996) 'The memory wars: Freud's legacy in dispute', *Journal of American Psychoanalytic Association*, 44: 573–9.

Miller, A. (1986) *Thou Shalt Not Be Aware: Society's Betrayal of the Child*. London: Virago.

Millett, K. (1970) *Sexual Politics*. New York: Doubleday.

Mitchell, J. (1974) *Psychoanalysis and Feminism*. London: Penguin Books.

Molnos, A. (1995) *A Question of Time: Essentials of Brief Dynamic Psychotherapy*. London: Karnac Books.

Momigliano, L.N. (1987) 'A spell in Vienna – but was Freud a Freudian? – an investigation into Freud's technique between 1920 and 1938, based on the published testimony of former analysands', *International Review of Psycho-Analysis*, 14: 373–89.

Obholzer, K. (1980) *The Wolf-Man*. London: Routledge and Kegan Paul.

O'Connor, N. and Ryan, J. (1993) *Wild Desires and Mistaken Identities: Lesbianism and Psychoanalysis*. London: Virago.

Orgel, S. (1996) 'Freud and the repudiation of the feminine', *Journal of the American Psychoanalytic Association*, 44S: 45–67.

Ornston, D.G. (ed.) (1992) *Translating Freud*. New Haven, CT: Yale University Press.

Person, E. and Ovesey, L. (1983) 'Psycho-analytic theories of gender identity', *Journal of the American Academy of Psychoanalysis*. 11(2): 203–26.

Popper, K. (1959) *The Logic of Scientific Discovery*. New York: Basic Books.

Rachman, S. and Wilson, G. (1980) *The Effects of Psychological Theory* (second edition). Oxford: Pergamon.

Racker, H. (1968) *Transference and Counter-Transference*. London: Hogarth Press.

Rainey, R.M. (1975) *Freud as Student of Religion: Perspective on the Background and Development of his Thought*. Missoula, MT: American Academy of Religion and Scholars' Press.

Rayner, E. (1991) *The Independent Mind in British Psychoanalysis*. Northvale, NJ: Jason Aronson.

162   *Sigmund Freud*

Ricoeur, P. (1970) *Freudian Philosophy: An Essay in Interpretation.* New Haven, CT: Yale University Press.

Rieff, P. (1959) *Freud: The Mind of a Moralist.* New York: Viking.

Rieff, P. (1973) *The Triumph of the Therapeutic.* London: Penguin Books.

Riviere, J. (1958) 'A character trait of Freud's', in J. Sutherland (ed.), *Psychoanalysis and Contemporary Thought.* London: Hogarth Press, pp. 145–9.

Roazen, P. (1979) *Freud and His Followers.* London: Penguin Books.

Rodman, F.R. (1987) *The Spontaneous Gesture: Selected Letters of D.W. Winnicott.* Cambridge, Mass.: Harvard University Press.

Roith, E. (1987) *The Riddle of Freud.* London: Tavistock Publications.

Roth, A. and Fonagy, P. (1996) *What Works for Whom? A Critical Review of Psychotherapy Research.* New York: Guilford.

Roudinesco, E. (1990) *Jacques Lacan and Co.: a History of Psychoanalysis in France, 1925–1985.* London: Free Association Books.

Rowan, J. and Jacobs, M. (2002) *The Therapist's Use of Self.* Buckingham: Open University Press.

Rubins, J. (1978) *Karen Horney: Gentle Rebel of Psychoanalysis.* London: Weidenfeld and Nicolson.

Runyan, W.M. (1982) *Life Histories and Psychobiography.* Oxford: Oxford University Press.

Rycroft, C. (1972) *A Critical Dictionary of Psychoanalysis.* London: Penguin Books.

Rycroft, C. (1985) *Psychoanalysis and Beyond.* London: Chatto and Windus.

Samuels, A. (ed.) (1985) *The Father: Contemporary Jungian Perspectives.* London: Free Association Books.

Sayers, J. (1991) *Mothering Psychoanalysis.* London: Hamish Hamilton.

Schafer, R. (1976) *A New Language for Psychoanalysis.* New Haven, CT: Yale University Press.

Schafer, R. (1983) *The Analytic Attitude.* New York: Basic Books.

Schermer, V.L. (1994) 'Between theory and practice, light and heat', in V.L. Schermer and M. Pines (eds), *Ring of Fire: Primitive Affects and Object Relations in Group Psychotherapy.* London: Routledge.

Segal, H. (1964) *Introduction to the Work of Melanie Klein.* London: Hogarth Press.

Segal, J. (1992) *Melanie Klein.* London: Sage Publications.

Stewart, I. (1992) *Eric Berne.* London: Sage Publications.

Symington, J. and Symington, N. (1996) *The Clinical Thinking of Wilfred Bion.* London: Routledge.

Thomas, D.M. (1981) *The White Hotel.* London: Penguin Books.

Thomas, D.M (1982) 'A fine romance'; review article, *New York Review of Books,* 29: 8.

Thorne, B. (2003) *Carl Rogers.* London: Sage Publications.

Tillich, P. (1957) *The Dynamics of Faith.* New York: Harper.

Turkle, S. (1979 *Psychoanalytic Politics: Freud's French Revolution.* London: Burnett

Wallis, K.C. and Poulton, J.L. (2001) *Internalization.* Buckingham: Open University Press.

Weinstein, F. (1980) 'On the social function of intellectuals', in M. Albin (ed.), *New Directions in Psychohistory.* Lexington, Mass.: Lexington Books.

Welchman, K. (2000) *Erik Erikson: His Life, Work and Significance.* Buckingham: Open University Press.

Winnicott, D.W. (1958) *Collected Papers: Through Paediatrics to Psychoanalysis*. London: Tavistock Publications.

Wisdom, J. (1963) *Psychoanalytic Technology*. London: Routledge and Kegan Paul.

Wollheim, R. (1971) *Freud*. Glasgow: Fontana/Collins.

Wright, E. (1984) *Psychoanalytic Criticism*. London: Methuen.

Yankura, J. and Dryden, W. (1994) *Albert Ellis*. London: Sage Publications.

Young-Bruehl, E. (1990) *Freud on Women*. London: Hogarth Press.

Index